Praise for Si

In every generation, theologic͟ ͟ ͟ versies have been expressed in the texts of hymns. Reading and studying these texts gives us a fascinating glimpse into history. Singing them today connects us to timeless Christian truths, as well as to the great cloud of witnesses from the distant past to the present day. It is this connection that makes it so essential to keep a wide selection of hymns in every congregation's repertoire. This book by Paul Rorem is a great, relatively quick read for anyone interested in the intersections of church history, theology, and church music. Recommended for seminarians as well as congregational book groups and Christian education courses.

—Tim Getz, director of music, Grace Lutheran
Church, Palo Alto, California

A brilliant idea brilliantly done! There is no book we can hold in our hand that contains as much history as a hymnal. The story of each hymn in its particularity can teach us moments in church history that, together, give us the entire sweep of the past from Miriam to Lina Sandell. A great treasure and resource for congregations.

—Gracia Grindal, professor emerita of rhetoric,
Luther Seminary

Hymns, songs, and liturgy are formational to our Lutheran faith, marrying music, poetry, and theology. Building on the work of Erik Routley and Paul Westermeyer, Rorem explores hymns and songs, old and new, revealing the way they reflect their time, both historically and theologically, and also transcend it. This new resource is an excellent way to bring pastors, musicians, and lay folks together to teach, learn about, and appreciate our singing history as the church of Jesus Christ.

—Julie Grindle, associate with the bishop of the Upstate
New York Synod of the ELCA, and church musician

Paul Rorem applies his deep knowledge of church history and theology to hymns, and the result is an engagingly written brief history of the subject. Intended for lay audiences, it would make a good college or seminary textbook.

—Joseph Herl, professor of music, Concordia
University, Seward, Nebraska

Hymnody has been referred to as a form of practical theology; the church's central beliefs about Jesus are expressed through what the church sings in worship. *Singing Church History* proves that point, introducing major events, theologies, and figures of Christian history through a breezy, eminently readable chronology of congregational song.

—Zebulon M. Highben, associate professor of the practice
of church music, Duke Divinity School, and director
of chapel music, Duke University Chapel

This is an unusual book, since we often associate hymns with worship, what we do on Sundays—those powerful songs that connect us with special times and special people in our lives. But as Paul Rorem creatively explores, the hymns we sing in the present also have a significant past. And it is in coming to terms with that past that our singing in the present takes on new meaning.

—Robin A. Leaver, professor emeritus, Westminster Choir College,
and editor of *A New Song We Now Begin: Celebrating
the Half Millennium of Lutheran Hymnals 1524–2024*

Paul Rorem's delightful book explains how well hymns illustrate the entire history of Christianity, but also how often hymns have played an active part in shaping that history. With full attention to the importance of Scripture for hymnody through the ages, illuminating portraits of key hymn writers, carefully crafted discussion questions, helpful appendices with hymns identified for liturgical and doctrinal use, and (not least) many hymns printed for singing, the book is well suited for both church and classroom. It is keyed to Lutheran hymnals, but thoroughly ecumenical in its coverage and usefulness.

—Mark Noll, professor emeritus, University of Notre Dame; coeditor of *Sing Them Over Again to Me: Hymns and Hymnbooks in America* and *Wonderful Words of Life: Hymns in American Protestant History and Theology*

Some people watch thrillers on TV. Even if they know the outcome, they enter into the event with an energy that puts them on the edge of their seat. Some people read mysteries and just can't put the book down. They keep that nightlight on through until they finish the next chapter . . . and then the next. Now Paul Rorem has given us a book that helps us to sing the faith that has been passed on to us in such a way that we not only come to love the church's history, but we can't wait to sing it again. Like the satisfaction we receive when we come to a final cadence of a robust hymn, Dr. Rorem has given us a joyous ride that will encourage us to keep singing with our congregations and our ecumenical neighbors, and with such singing, the life of church will flourish.

—Amy C. Schifrin, president emeritus, North American Lutheran Seminary; associate professor of liturgy and homiletics (retired), Trinity School for Ministry

This book scans the history of the Christian church by means of hymns. In the process, it provides theological and historical insights. It is a valuable resource for scholars, teachers, church musicians, and others who seek to understand the church and its song.

—Paul Westermeyer, emeritus professor of church music, cantor, and director of MSM degree program with St. Olaf College, Luther Seminary, St. Paul, Minnesota

Paul Rorem tells the story of the Christian church through hymn texts dating from the first centuries of the church's existence to the present day. Simultaneously, he provides the reader with welcome insights to these texts. His historical and geographical scope is commendably broad, with welcome attention to early and medieval hymn texts as well as global hymnody from the mid-twentieth century to the present. He has that rare gift of writing in a highly accessible way while not glossing over sometimes difficult historical issues.

—Dr. Daniel Zager, librarian emeritus,
Eastman School of Music

SINGING
CHURCH
HISTORY

PAUL ROREM

SINGING

CHURCH

HISTORY

INTRODUCING THE CHRISTIAN STORY
THROUGH HYMN TEXTS

Fortress Press
Minneapolis

SINGING CHURCH HISTORY
Introducing the Christian Story through Hymn Texts

Library of Congress Cataloging-in-Publication Data

Names: Rorem, Paul, author.
Title: Singing church history : introducing the Christian story through
   hymn texts / Paul Rorem.
Description: Minneapolis : Fortress Press, 2024. | Includes bibliographical
   references and index.
Identifiers: LCCN 2023041736 (print) | LCCN 2023041737 (ebook) | ISBN
   9781506496214 (paperback) | ISBN 9781506496238 (ebook)
Subjects: LCSH: Hymns--History and criticism. | Church music. | Church
   history. | Hymn writers.
Classification: LCC ML3086 .R67 2024 (print) | LCC ML3086 (ebook) | DDC
   782.2709--dc23eng/20230913
LC record available at https://lccn.loc.gov/2023041736
LC ebook record available at https://lccn.loc.gov/2023041737

Cover design: John Lucas
Cover photos: Ambrose of Milan: Detail from mosaic of Saint Ambrose in the dome
of the shrine of San Vittore in ciel d'oro, now a chapel of Sant'Ambrogio basilica,
5th century; John of Damascus: Painting of John of Damascus, St Nicholas Russian
Orthodox Church, Dallas Texas; Luther: Portrait of Martin Luther (1483–1546), by
Lucas Cranach the Elder, 1526, Nationalmuseum, Stockholm, Sweden; Philipp Nicolai:
Portrait of Hymn writer Philipp Nicolai, 17th century commemorative engraving made
after his death in 1608; Fannie Crosby: Photo of Fannie Crosby, 1900, Bain News Service
photograph collection (Library of Congress, USA); James Weldon Johnson: James Weldon
Johnson, half-length portrait at desk with telephone, 1900, Visual Materials from the
NAACP Records collection (Library of Congress, USA)

Print ISBN: 978-1-5064-9621-4
eBook ISBN: 978-1-5064-9623-8

For Annie, Joe, and hymn leaders everywhere

CONTENTS

PREFACE

Hymns were the formative soundtrack of my childhood, a common yet precious experience. At Zion Lutheran Church in Appleton, Minnesota, I sang hymns with my parents, including some they knew from my Norwegian-American grandparents. Later, as Pastor of Our Savior's Lutheran Church in Edison, New Jersey, I embraced the challenge of choosing the hymns that might influence a congregation and its members, young and old. Along the way I learned from my Doktorvater Karlfried Froehlich that a great way into Martin Luther's theology was through his hymn texts. When I started teaching church history, I diversified a few lectures by adding some familiar hymns from early, medieval, and Reformation contexts. Students at first thought it odd to sing a hymn in the middle of a class, but they soon expected it (and benefited unawares from the renewal of their oxygen levels). A separate course grew from there, and later I also ventured into early modern and American church history, team-teaching a survey course with Martin Tel, the C. F. Seabrook Director of Music at Princeton Theological Seminary. Outside of my family, this book's greatest debts are to Karlfried Froehlich, still my mentor, to Martin Tel, co-teacher and key consultant, and to the students in those courses. Above all, I thank my wife Kate Skrebutenas for her support, patience, and sharp eye in reading all of this.

Other friends and colleagues have commented helpfully on various sections of this project, including Matthew Becker, Lorraine Brugh, Heath Carter, Matthew Carver, Boyd Coolman, Mark Dixon, Philip Forness, Allie Graham-Hicks, Mary Jane Haemig, Joseph Herl, Nicholas Hopman, Nancy Koester, Nina Laubach, Robin Leaver, Swee Hong Lim, Mark Mattes, Ruth Naomi, Carl P. E. Springer, Patricia Stewart,

Timothy Wengert, and Paul Westermeyer whose *Hymnal Companion to Evangelical Lutheran Worship* has been immensely helpful.

Laura Gifford and a Fortress team of colleagues have shaped the basic text into this illustrated resource with helpful patience, wisdom, and an eye for how it will look to the reader. A project like this needs to choose a specific hymnal for consistency of reference. Although readers from any denominational background should find this historical overview helpful, its choice of *Evangelical Lutheran Worship* fits the author's context, the publisher's affiliation, and the realities of copyright permissions.

After drafting the text, I came across Robert C. Mann's *The Church Sings Its Faith* (Chicago: GIA Publications, 2022), a history of hymnody with more focus on the music and less on historical context—especially the premodern materials of my teaching specialty. Those looking for more coverage of modern hymnody can profitably consult Mann's book. Similarly, I belatedly realized that I may have been influenced early on by Mark Noll's *Turning Points: Decisive Moments in the History of Christianity*, since he often cited a hymn as illustrative of a movement or era.

Last, here's to all the church musicians who choose, play, and lead hymns in Christian communities of all kinds. This project concentrates on the words, as a way into church history, but only with the music are hymns so deeply, mysteriously formative, creating memories, nurturing faith, and shaping communal ties. As Martin Luther said, music is a gift from God.

So, the song goes on. This book is dedicated to our daughter Annie, who at first sang better than she spoke, to our son Joe, who added the bass notes, and to hymn leaders everywhere, from Zion in Appleton to Princeton Seminary and wherever its students may yet go.

Paul Rorem
Princeton, NJ
August 2023

1

PRELUDE

"Alleluia, Amen"

SUNDAY MORNINGS WE sing words that have a history, texts that document our shared history as Christians. We are singing church history; and, as a singing church, we have a history. This book tells that story. It introduces church history by way of hymn texts, and it seeks to enrich our hymn singing with glimpses into the lives and contexts of those who wrote them. Since hymns have come down to us from specific situations, such texts can lead us back into those contexts, back into Christian history. A single phrase from a familiar hymn can point to a major historical movement or controversy, just as an author's life story can illuminate his or her hymns.

The category of "hymns" will here be very broad, including various types of congregational singing such as Psalms and canticles, spirituals and gospel songs, even the sung portions of the liturgy. This includes some ancient or medieval poetry that was not sung corporately at the time but was translated and set to music centuries later.

Some such hymn texts are quite old, surprisingly old especially if the tunes sound modern. They are often translations from ancient texts, sources such as the Bible itself of course, but also historic Christian literature in Latin or Greek. Furthermore, many modern hymn texts are English translations, not from antiquity but from German and other European languages, and from vibrant Christian communities today in Africa, East Asia, and Latin America.

The texts we sing thus give us Scripture, Christian history, *and* worldwide Christianity. Yet many of these hymns are so familiar musically that we rarely notice where the words come from. Favorite tunes and stirring settings are essential to singing church history, uniting body and soul in communal Christian formation. Indeed, the music helps us remember the words so that we can sing together, not just listen to some leaders. Still, this book pays particular attention not to the music but to the texts, for they provide both information and formation. We can leave the music to others, with appreciation for their expertise. Here, it is the words that open up our shared history and the Christian message.

The Big Picture

The main source of texts sung in church is the Bible, in several ways. Over time, the Psalms became a major font for such singing. We all recognize Psalm 23, but we also sing many other Psalm verses or paraphrases, often without recognizing the source. Perhaps we know that Luther's "Mighty Fortress" starts with a nod to Psalm 46, or that Isaac Watts was paraphrasing Psalm 90 with "O God, Our Help in Ages Past." But, that "Jesus Shall Reign" comes from a Psalm (72) or even "Joy to the World" (98)!? Christians have also sung biblical canticles through the centuries, such as the "Song of Miriam" (Exodus 15) and Mary's *Magnificat* (Luke 1). Further, several of the texts sung most often in Christian history, namely, in the liturgy, also come from Scripture. "*Kyrie*; Lord, Have Mercy" comes from Matthew 15 (and 17 and 20), "Glory to God in the Highest" from Luke 2, "Holy, Holy, Holy" from Isaiah 6, and "Lamb of God" from John 1. From this same wellspring of the Bible flowed centuries of other sung texts around the world, whether translations or paraphrases or new poetic expressions of the biblical message.

Building on the biblical basis, the structure of this book is chronological, from the early Christian centuries through history to today. In the early church, a big controversy over Christ's divinity led to the Nicene Creed and to some Latin texts stressing Christ as fully

God, such as Ambrose's hymn "Savior of the Nations, Come" and Prudentius's poem "Of the Father's Love Begotten." The Greek side of the story reflects the Orthodox Church, with its liturgical riches ("Let All Mortal Flesh Keep Silence") and theological giants like the eighth-century John of Damascus ("Come, You Faithful, Raise the Strain"). There is also a rich treasury of Syriac hymnody in other Eastern Orthodox churches, but little of it appears in modern hymnals.

In the Western Middle Ages, Benedictine monks and nuns sang the Psalms and Latin hymns across Europe, including the *Te Deum,* "Holy God, We Praise Your Name." Such elegant texts can help refute the myth of the "Dark" Ages. Famous medieval figures were also hymn writers. In the twelfth century, Bernard of Clairvaux's works were turned to song, and a follower expressed these sentiments in "O Sacred Head, Now Wounded." Francis of Assisi inspired many fanciful legends, but he really did write "The Canticle of Brother Sun," often sung today as "All Creatures of Our God and King." Thomas Aquinas may be more famous for his large summaries of theology in the thirteenth century, but he also wrote sacramental poetry, as in "Thee We Adore." There are many other medieval hymns in wide use today, perhaps to Protestant surprise. Late medieval spirituality, as in "Oh, Love, How Deep, How Broad, How High" from the Modern Devotion of Thomas à Kempis in the fifteenth century, was one of several "reforms before the Reformation."

So we come to the familiar era of Protestant hymnody and to the first hymnals in 1524. Martin Luther paraphrased not only some Psalms and the liturgy into singable German but also some of the texts he received from the medieval tradition. In fact, most "Luther hymns" start with inherited texts. Besides Scripture, some of them reinforce the basic Christian catechism: the Ten Commandments, the Lord's Prayer, the Creed, Baptism, and the Lord's Supper. He wrote a few new ones too. One of them gives an overview of the whole Christian message, including his own experience: "Dear Christians, One and All, Rejoice." The Reformed tradition, especially the Geneva Psalter, centered Presbyterian attention on the Psalms, such as what became known as OLD HUNDREDTH ("All People That On Earth Do Dwell").

From the seventeenth century onward, Christian history features so many familiar hymn texts that key eras and movements can have only one or two representatives here. Amid a horrific plague, Philipp Nicolai's 1599 duo provides an early sampler: "Wake, Awake" and "O Morning Star." The spiritual poetry of what became known as Pietism warmed hearts across countries, languages, and confessional borders, and it still does. Moravian Pietist hymnody influenced Sweden, for example, and especially England by way of the Wesley brothers. Charles Wesley's immense output is represented here by his familiar "Love Divine, All Loves Excelling" (1747), with some wording that was controversial within the Methodist movement. Wesleyan song then rang through the American colonies and into the multiple revival movements of the United States, such as Fanny Crosby's popular "Blessed Assurance" in 1873. Pietist sentiments also shaped Walter Rauschenbusch, the theologian of the "Social Gospel" whose Baptist legacy was carried deep into the twentieth century by Harry Emerson Fosdick ("God of Grace and God of Glory," 1931). African Americans also sang the Wesleyan revival songs but had their own spirituals and even an anthem, "Lift Every Voice and Sing" (1900). Thomas A. Dorsey added "Precious Lord, Take My Hand" in 1932 from his personal heartache.

Lastly, and currently, "World Christianity" refers to worldwide and ecumenical Christian song from around the globe, especially Africa, East Asia, and Latin America, with translations into and from European languages. Further, venerable Latin (*Veni Sancte Spiritus*) and even biblical Greek (*Kyrie*) are making comebacks as ways to transcend language barriers, in Taizé and its offshoots. As throughout history, hymn texts are again cross-cultural resources that can link diverse churches together.

Besides guiding us into Christian history, as in this basic narrative, hymn texts also accompany us through the church year, teach us basic Christian doctrine, and increase ecumenical awareness. Added to this book's chronological flow are suggestions of the hymns that could also enrich the seasons of the year from Advent through Pentecost, or introduce basic doctrines from creation through Christology to eschatology, or open up church traditions worldwide, both Orthodox and Roman Catholic, Lutheran and Anglican, Methodist and Evangelical, with Pentecostal and non-denominational movements as well.

All in all, our basic repertoire of sung texts can lead us into Scripture and history, plus the wide array of global Christianity's liturgical, doctrinal, and ecumenical riches.

Psalms, Canticles, and Other Biblical Refrains

As with Christian history in general, the history of our sung texts can be approached as an aspect of the history of biblical interpretation. Individual Hebrew words such as *Alleluia* and *Amen* plus Greek phrases such as *Kyrie eleison* ("Lord, Have Mercy") are biblical anchors in Christian singing, and many hymns loosely paraphrase some Psalm portions. Furthermore, even hymns newly written without explicit scriptural citations are also based on the biblical message.[1]

The category of "hymns," both in the Bible and in general, needs clarification. The ancient world, whether Greco-Roman or Israelite or early Christian, featured many poetic texts sometimes called hymns, but they were not meant for communal song. Such poetry abounds as literature in Latin, Greek, and other ancient languages. It was usually meant to be spoken aloud or even chanted by a soloist, but not sung

---

1   See the extensive scriptural index in Paul Westermeyer's valuable *Hymnal Companion to Evangelical Lutheran Worship* (Minneapolis: Augsburg Fortress, 2010), 857–872, to be cited as *ELW Companion*. See also the index to the *Lutheran Service Book* (St. Louis: Concordia Publishing House, 2006), to be cited as LSB, and the extensive biblical and historical detail in the *Lutheran Service Book Companion to the Hymns*, ed. J. Herl, P. C. Reske, and J. D. Vieker, 2 vols. (St. Louis: Concordia Publishing House, 2019), to be cited as *LSB Companion* with the hymn number, or vol. 2 and page numbers for the essays.

by the whole community. Indeed, a solo lector chanting the Gospel lesson meant a sung text, originally for acoustic reasons, but this is not a congregational hymn. Some of the biblical poetry became true hymnody only centuries later, but there is ample scriptural precedent for singing in groups.

Within the Bible, singing the faith is consistently modeled as a core activity of the people of God, from the early Exodus through the Psalms and the Gospels to the final Revelation. Perhaps the earliest example is the canticle or "ode" called the "Song of Miriam" in Exodus 15, sung upon God's triumph for Israel at the Red Sea. "Sing to the Lord, for he has triumphed gloriously; horse and rider he has thrown into the sea." Among others, John of Damascus picked up on this theme in his Easter hymn "Come, You Faithful, Raise the Strain."[2] At the end of the Bible, the Revelation to John is packed with heavenly hymns, "singing a new song," . . . "singing with full voice" and "they sing the song of Moses, the servant of God, and the song of the Lamb" (Revelation 5 and 15; see "This is the Feast," ELW 165–66).

The Psalter is a special case, and more will be said about singing the Psalms in the following chapters. After all, not only King David but also Jesus and his disciples, including St. Paul, sang the Psalms (Matthew 26:30 and Mark 14:26, with Ephesians 5:19 and Colossians 3:16; see also 1 Corinthians 14), thus providing royal and divine warrant along with apostolic precedent. Early monastic communities led the way, as seen in the Benedictine model of singing through all the Psalms every week. Modern hymnals abound in familiar renditions of Psalm 23 (ELW 502, 778, 780, 782, 789), but other famous hymns are also taken directly from the Psalter. Luther's "Out of the Depths" (ELW 600) is really Psalm 130; the Geneva Psalter is sung regularly,

---

2   *Evangelical Lutheran Worship* (Minneapolis: Augsburg Fortress, 2006), 363; henceforth, ELW. See also "At the Lamb's High Feast We Sing" (ELW 362, st. 3b): "Israel's hosts triumphant go through the wave that drowns the foe."

especially "All People That on Earth Do Dwell" (OLD HUNDREDTH, ELW 883); Isaac Watt's "O God, Our Help in Ages Past" (ELW 632) is a version of Psalm 90. Generations of Lutherans have sung "Create in Me a Clean Heart, O God," often to the old tune in J. A. Freylinghausen's 1704 hymnal (ELW 188), perhaps only later to realize that this comes from Psalm 51. Such examples abound.

The second great collection of biblical songs that have become the church's hymnody comes under the heading of "canticles" or "odes," led by Luke's nativity narrative. Mary's famous *Magnificat* (Luke 1, "My Soul Proclaims the Greatness of the Lord") is known in multiple versions (ELW, pp. 314–15 for Morning Prayer, ELW 234–36, 251, 573, 723, and 882; LSB 925–38). Zechariah's *Benedictus* (also Luke 1, "Blessed be the Lord God of Israel") is a standard part of Morning Prayer as well as several hymns (ELW, p. 303, with ELW 226, 250, 552). The Song of Simeon from Luke 2 (*Nunc dimittis*, "Now Let Your Servant Depart in Peace") is also familiar from multiple contexts such as the communion liturgy, Compline (ELW, p. 324), ELW 200–04 and 313, as well as Luther's paraphrase (ELW 440). Of course, Christmas carols galore also stem from the birth accounts in Luke and Matthew. There are also canticles from other parts of Scripture, such as the Song of Miriam, as mentioned earlier; see ELW "Service Music" 151–238. The Orthodox tradition identifies several of them from the Old Testament: the Song of Moses (Deuteronomy 32), the Prayer of Hannah (I Samuel 2), the Prayer of Habakkuk (Habakkuk 3, LSB 986), the Prayer of Isaiah (Isaiah 26), and the Prayer of Jonah (Jonah 2).

There are other New Testament texts sometimes called hymns. St. Paul's words of praise for and to Christ in Philippians 2 and Colossians 1, along with the opening of John's Gospel, have struck some modern biblical scholars as hymn-like, perhaps even citing prior texts that were sung in earliest Christian worship. Other scholars argue that even if these texts are special units of poetic composition, there is no evidence that they were actually sung by worshipping communities, whether before or after the New Testament. The debate continues, but it has little to do with our topic. Unlike the Psalms or the New Testament canticles such as the *Magnificat* or the *Gloria in excelsis*, these "Christological hymns" do not appear in the overall history of hymnody as congregational song but only in recent biblical scholarship.[3]

The biblical phrases that have been sung and heard most often in Christian history, however, are not from the Psalms or the canticles, whether Old or New Testament, but the scriptural portions of the liturgy said or sung weekly or even daily across the centuries. Called the "Ordinary" of the Mass in the Latin tradition because it is always there every time in every season, these biblical quotations can be simple sentences spoken or sung, or longer texts sometimes set to elaborate music for special performances such as Vivaldi's "Gloria" or J. S. Bach's "B Minor Mass." They start simply with the Greek *Kyrie* ("Lord, have mercy") said in one version by the Canaanite woman in Matthew 15 and then in the familiar *Kyrie eleison* of Matthew 17 and 20. Variations like "Lord, have mercy; Christ, have mercy" appear in ELW Service Music 151–58. Next comes the Latin *Gloria in excelsis*, quoting the angels in Luke 2, "Glory to God in the Highest" (ELW 162–64) with some additional phrases both biblical ("Lamb of God," see below) and traditional. As for hymnic variations, see the paraphrase by Luther's student Nikolaus Decius, "All Glory Be to God on High" (ELW 410, with inclusion in ELW setting 5, p. 159, and LSB 947), plus of course "Angels We Have Heard on High" (ELW 289 and LSB 368). Although the Hebrew *Alleluia* sung before the Gospel was not really part of the Ordinary, being variable and omitted in Lent, it was an important feature of the Mass, especially because it was often expanded into a hymn of sorts called a "sequence."

The communion liturgy itself early on featured the *Sanctus*, "Holy, Holy, Holy, Lord God of power and might, heaven and earth are full of

3   See also 1 Timothy 3:16, 6:15–16, and other texts. For a summary of these issues, see Matthew E. Gordley, *New Testament Christological Hymns* (Downers Grove, IL: IVP Academic, 2018).

your glory," from Isaiah 6 and expanded in Revelation 4.[4] Attached to
the *Sanctus* is the *Benedictus*, from the Palm Sunday account in Matthew 21:9, quoting Psalm 118: "Blessed is he who comes in the Name
of the Lord." Finally, the *Agnus Dei*, "Lamb of God, you take away the
sin of the world," comes from John the Baptist's confession in John 1,
and it is also partially embedded in the *Gloria* earlier in the Ordinary.
Its conclusion is familiar, too: *Dona nobis pacem* ("Grant us peace").
Beyond the set Ordinary of every Mass, the variable "Propers" were
basically taken from Scripture as well, such as the Psalm verses sung
in the Introit (entrance) or in the Gradual (transition to the Gospel
lesson).

Overall, from the full-text use of Psalms and canticles to the
phrases in the liturgy and even the mere words *Alleluia* and *Amen*, the
basic source of words for Christian singing is the Bible. As we look
through Christian history, we will also see that most hymns are based
on scriptural content, whether direct quotations or loose paraphrases
or at least subtle allusions.

---

4   ELW 189–93, with ELW 413 and Luther's own paraphrase, "Isaiah in a Vision
Did of Old," ELW 868 and LSB 960. For an early witness, around 100 CE, see Clement's first letter to Corinth, 34.6–7.

2

THE EARLY CHURCH, WESTERN AND LATIN (100–500)

"Praise we sing to Christ the Lord"

AFTER THE WEALTH of the biblical hymnody, especially the vast concluding array of sung texts in the Revelation to John, the next century's lack of material can come as a disappointment. What strikes us first is the silence: there is hardly any mention of singing at all, not even of the Psalms. In general, the second century into the third has so few Christian documents of any kind that we should not be surprised to find scant mention of singing. A Roman governor's report around 110 CE gives a tantalizing shard of evidence: "at dawn," Pliny reported to Emperor Trajan, "they sing a song (*carmen*) to Christ as to a god."[1] Whether Christ is a god, or God, or not, will come up again!

The "Apostolic Fathers," meaning those few writings between the biblical apostles and the church writers so numerous later, do give tiny glimpses of Christian worship, but they rarely mention singing, not even the Psalter. Around 100 CE, the *Didache* (Teaching) records some prayers at baptism and the communion service, but there is no mention of singing. However, its poetic prayer over the bread (*Didache* 9), including the scattered grain "gathered into one" like the unity of the church, has inspired some modern hymnody ("As the Grains of

---

1   *Carmen Christo quasi deo dicere*; Pliny, *Epistulae* X.96, in *Readings in World Christian History, Vol. I, Earliest Christianity to 1453*, ed. John W. Coakley and Andrea Sterk (Maryknoll, New York: Orbis Books, 2004), 23–24. To be cited as *Readings*, Coakley and Sterk.

Wheat," ELW 465, see also ELW 478 and LSB 652). As we shall see, many of our hymns are settings of poetic texts that were originally not for group singing.

The second Christian century has very little pertinent evidence. The most important witness is Justin Martyr (ca. 100—ca. 165) who described the Sunday assembly in terms of scripture readings, sermon, prayers, and the meal, but with no reference to hymns or singing of any kind. Elsewhere (*First Apology* 13 and 67) he mentioned "solemn prayers and hymns," but gave no examples. With their echoes of the Psalms and all the "Alleluias," the "Odes of Solomon" may be songs from this period, but there is no evidence that they were sung in Christian worship. Similarly, the "Gnostics" had hymns, as seen in the miscellany called *Pistis Sophia,* but they did not enter into general use.

The third century is also short of texts, in general and as to singing and hymnody, but here the story can at least resume. In the Latin half of the Roman Empire, Tertullian around 200 CE (*On Prayer* 25, 27) mentioned that Christians sang Psalms and hymns at home and at church. In Alexandria, the Greek center in Egypt, a large body of third-century literature includes a text pertinent to hymnody. Clement of Alexandria (ca. 150–ca. 215) was a famous Christian teacher, as seen in his major philosophical-theological works, including catechetical pedagogy. To one of these works, aptly called *The Teacher* (or Tutor, for *Paedagogus*), he appended a poem about Christ as a teacher. It refers to singing, but was it sung as a hymn? It appears in some modern hymnals as "Shepherd of Tender Youth," from the free translation of a small portion in the nineteenth century by Henry M. Dexter (LSB 864; another loose paraphrase is by H. M. McGill). For Clement it was a teaching tool, nicely summing up much of the longer work it accompanied, but there is no evidence that it was sung in his time or thereafter. The length and the textual complexity of Clement's poem, full of classical Greek allusions, argue against its use in communal singing. Further, Clement himself in this same work warned against singing inappropriately as the Greeks and the Romans do.[2]

The lack of evidence for congregational singing in earliest Christianity fits the overall gaps in our knowledge about that era of Christian history. But Clement's caution points to another factor. Clearly there was a lot of singing in the ancient world, such as drinking songs. Besides Clement, other early texts such as the third-century *Didascalia* sternly warn Christians about the immorality and idolatry associated with singing in general. Generally, the evidence from the second and third Christian centuries is scarce, whether of texts that might have been sung or of arguments for or against such singing. That there was hymn singing in these centuries is asserted confidently by Eusebius in his fourth-century *Ecclesiastical History*, chapter 5, and, as Pliny had reported earlier, they sang "of Christ as the Word of God and address him as God."

On the Psalms in particular, the lack of early evidence for singing them does not mean they were neglected. Like other parts of the Old Testament, and as seen all through the New Testament, Psalm texts were central to the early church's theological pattern of prophecy and fulfillment: what was anticipated in the Psalms was fulfilled in Christ. Singing the Psalms becomes well-documented as the third century turns into the fourth, initially not in the Sunday assembly but rather in the daily prayers of the emerging monastic communities. With testimonies from Pachomius and Athanasius in the East, plus travelers to and from the West like Cassian and Egeria, it is clear that singing the Psalms and lots of them became a common practice for ascetic communities of men or women. From usage day and night in the monastic context, the singing of certain Psalms spread to special services and Sunday worship in congregational life.[3] As we shall see,

---

2   *Paed.* 2.4.43–44; on Clement's poetic text, see Matthew E. Gordley, *Teaching through Song in Antiquity* (Tübingen: Mohr Siebeck, 2011), 371–381.

3   For the limited use of the Psalms in early Christian worship, see the accessible introduction in Paul Bradshaw, *Two Ways of Prayer* (Nashville: Abingdon, 1995), 73–87;

Bishop Ambrose led his church in Milan to sing the Psalms in the late fourth century and, later, Benedict instructed his monks to sing all one hundred and fifty Psalms every week.[4]

This situation of slim textual evidence changed dramatically in the fourth century, both for Psalm singing and also for multiple sung texts not directly from Scripture. The reason the fourth century contains so much more Christian literature, including evidence of worship orders and examples of hymnody, is clear. Emperor Constantine's edict in 313 CE ended the "Great Persecution" of Diocletian (303–11) and began an era of support for a more public or open Christian church. Early evidence of this new pattern was the Council of Nicaea in 325, called and funded by Constantine to iron out some differences among his Christian subjects and thus to solidify unity in the empire. The Nicene Creed, as known in the expanded version from the Council of Constantinople in 381, leads us directly into the early history of Christian hymnody. The disputed subject was Christ: Is he really God? A priest named Arius argued that Christ was the Savior, the first-born of creation sent by God, but not really the eternal God himself. There was, Arius seemed to say, (a time) when Christ was not. To support his views, he wrote some hymns for his followers to sing, such as the "Thalia." Others, however, insisted that Christ was "Very God from Very God," as the Creed put it, "of one Being with the Father through whom all things were made." Arius and his large following eventually lost out, and their hymns were lost too. But the controversy raged for generations. On the one hand, it heightened the concern that singing texts outside of Scripture can lead the faithful away from true doctrine;

---

for more depth and detail, see Karlfried Froehlich, "Discerning the Voices: Praise and Lament in the Tradition of the Christian Psalter," *Calvin Theological Journal* 36 (2001): 75–90.

4   Jim Samra, "Hymns and Creedal Worship in the New Testament," *Hymns and Hymnody, Historical and Theological Introductions, Vol. 1, From Asia Minor to Western Europe*, ed. Mark A. Lamport, Benjamin K. Forrest, and Vernon M. Whaley (Eugene, OR: Cascade Books, 2019), 22–23. To be cited as *Hymns and Hymnody*, vol. 1.

on the other hand, the Nicene position on Christ's full divinity soon found its own way into multiple hymns, including some that became famous through the centuries.

The Nicene Creed

We believe in one God,
   the Father, the Almighty,
   maker of heaven and earth,
   of all that is, seen and unseen.
We believe in one Lord, Jesus Christ,
   the only Son of God,
   eternally begotten of the Father,
   God from God, Light from Light,
   true God from true God,
   begotten, not made,
   of one Being with the Father;
   through him all things were made.
For us and for our salvation
      he came down from heaven,
      was incarnate of the Holy Spirit and the virgin
         Mary
      and became truly human.
      For our sake he was crucified under Pontius
         Pilate;
      he suffered death and was buried.
      On the third day he rose again
      in accordance with the scriptures;
      he ascended into heaven
      and is seated at the right hand of the Father.
      He will come again in glory to judge the living
         and the dead,
      and his kingdom will have no end.
We believe in the Holy Spirit, the Lord, the giver of life,

> *who proceeds from the Father and the Son,*[5]
> *who with the Father and the Son is worshiped and*
>   *glorified,*
> *who has spoken through the prophets.*
> *We believe in one holy catholic and apostolic church.*
> *We acknowledge one baptism for the forgiveness of*
>   *sins.*
> *We look for the resurrection of the dead,*
>   *and the life of the world to come. Amen.*

In the eastern Greek part of the Roman Empire, the Arian view of the Trinity (Christ as lesser than the Father) battled with the Nicene view for half a century, until the Council of Constantinople in 381 reaffirmed the Son as "of the same being" (*homo-ousion*) as the Father, and added a strong paragraph about the Holy Spirit, leading to the legal outlawing and banishment of the Arian sympathizers. The Son and the Holy Spirit were not separate beings but God's *self*-expressions as God's Word and God's Spirit. In the Western or Latin end of the empire, however, where some of the Arian communities thrived in exile across the borders as missionaries to the Germanic tribes, the controversy continued for several centuries. Hilary of Poitiers apparently wrote a few hymns around 360 CE against the Arians, some of the very first hymns in Latin, but only small fragments remain. Other Latin Fathers, like Ambrose of Milan and Augustine of Hippo, battled the subordination of Christ for most of their careers, and hymns were key factors in that battle.

For hymn texts outside of Scripture, the abundant material can be divided into Latin and Greek examples. Early Latin hymnody, starting in the fourth century, relates directly to the doctrinal controversy that produced the Nicene Creed in that era: namely, was Christ really God? Early Greek hymnody, taken up in the next chapter, echoes fragments of ancient liturgical traditions. Other early texts such as Syriac

---

5   The phrase "and the Son" is a later addition to the creed, to be discussed in chapter 4.

poetry, also in the next chapter, will lead us to important early church communities and resources, but they were rarely tapped in the overall history of Western hymnody that is our main subject.

Ambrose of Milan (ca. 339–97)

Ambrose of Milan

When we with Ambrose sing of "Very God and Mary's son," it is no coincidence that this translation of "Savior of the Nations, Come" follows the Nicene Creed quite closely. One of the giant figures of early Christian history, Ambrose of Milan was first a lawyer and then the Roman governor of the area around Milan, Italy. Amid disputes between the Nicene and Arian Christians there, before the Council of Constantinople ruled on the matter in 381, the beleaguered populace acclaimed governor Ambrose as their ecclesial leader even though he was still an unbaptized catechumen (inquirer). Within a single week in Advent of 374 he was then baptized, ordained as priest, and installed as bishop, the envy of impatient ministerial candidates ever since. With his government experience he could stand up to the emperor, calling him to account and to repentance for his misdeeds. With his wide reading, he knew how to oppose the Arians, including in his hymnody as we shall see. From his familiarity with some Eastern Church customs and writings, such as Clement and Origen of Alexandria, he taught and preached the spiritual meaning of the Scriptures. Most specifically, Ambrose promoted the antiphonal or alternating singing of the Psalms, as he learned it from Greek Christians like Basil the Great. Augustine himself was deeply affected by Ambrose the preacher and records in his *Confessions* (9.7.15; see also 9.4.8) how the bishop used the eastern custom of antiphonal Psalm singing to rally congregational convictions against the Arians.

Following his eastern near-contemporaries like Basil, Ambrose sang the praises of the Psalms not merely as texts but especially as texts to be sung. He praised music itself because it "delights the ear and softens the soul." Augustine and others worried that the beauty of the tune could distract from the truth of the text (*Confessions* 10), but Ambrose shared in the delight of the musical experience:

> *Old men ignore the stiffness of age to sing a psalm. . . . Young men sing one without the bane of lust. . . . Young women sing Psalms with no loss of wifely decency . . . and the child who refuses to learn other things takes pleasure in contemplating it. . . . A psalm is sung by emperors and rejoiced in by the people. . . . A psalm is sung at home and repeated outdoors; it is learned without effort and retained with delight.*[6]

More to our point, Ambrose wrote new hymns, as Augustine testified and as well documented in general. The dozen known hymns that Ambrose himself wrote come in three groups: hymns for different hours of the day, hymns for highlights of the church year, and hymns for martyrs. The first category includes a morning hymn that illustrates the overall anti-Arian purpose of his hymnody, and the second group features the Advent hymn that confirms it. As with his other hymns, "O Splendor of God's Glory Bright" (ELW 559 and LSB 874, *Splendor*

---

6   Brian P. Dunkle, SJ, *Enchantment and Creed in the Hymns of Ambrose of Milan* (Oxford: Oxford University Press, 2016), 43, quoting Ambrose on Psalm 119 (CSEL 62.3), then on Psalm 1 (CSEL 64.280). To be cited as Dunkle, *Ambrose*.

paternae gloriae) promotes the Nicene view of Christ's full divinity in a meter and a text designed for congregational singing. Taken from the opening line, the title itself reflects Hebrews 1; Christ is the splendid light or "reflection of God's glory." The second line echoes the Nicene Creed quite exactly: Christ as "light from light." The anti-Arian point is made explicit in conclusion, although modern versions drop this part. The original text ends with a striking statement of "the whole Son in the Father, and the whole Father in the Word,"[7] something the Arians could never say or sing. Lutheran hymnals drop this stanza, but by adding their own variations on the traditional and trinitarian doxology (*Gloria Patri*) the same point is made, although subtly. Ambrose also had a trinitarian doxology close his other famous hymn, *Deus, creator omnium*, "O God, Creator of all things." This hymn, affirming the goodness of creation, comforted Augustine when his mother died (*Confessions* 9.12.32, and elsewhere).

Singing "Glory be to the Father and to the Son," etc. (the *Gloria Patri*) may seem to modern ears a routine way to conclude a Psalm or a hymn, and indeed Benedict's *Rule* in the sixth century refers to it that way, but here too the background is polemical. The Arians, according to a later account, sang "Glory *to* the Father *through* the Son *in* the Holy Spirit," thus keeping Son and Spirit separate from and lower than the supreme Father. But the Nicene way did not use those different prepositions. Singing "Glory *to* the Father and *to* the Son and *to* the Holy Spirit" ascribes supreme honor and divinity to God equally in all three persons. Also, singing "as it was in the beginning" affirms that there never was (a time) when Christ was not. Small distinctions made a big difference, as with the one "iota of difference" between the Nicene confession of *homo-ousion* (same being) and the variation *homoi* (similar) as the Milanese Arians or Homoians preferred.

---

7   *in Patre totus Filius, et totus in Verbo Pater,* Dunkle, *Ambrose,* appendix 2, 222. LSB 874 has six stanzas, from the Bridges translation, but also lacks the Ambrosian finale. See also "O Trinity, O Blessed Light," ELW 571 and LSB 890.

"Savior of the Nations, Come" (ELW 263, LSB 332)

There are other authentic Ambrosian hymns to make this point, plus the much later legend that when Ambrose baptized Augustine in 387 the two of them spontaneously created the *Te Deum,* but the most influential hymn by Ambrose is "Savior of the Nations, Come." Martin Luther translated Ambrose's text (*Veni, Redemptor gentium*) as *Nun Komm, der Heiden Heiland* and congregations ever since have sung various translations as an Advent hymn. As with his hymns for Epiphany and Easter, here Ambrose applies the biblical witness to the emerging church year with creativity but in service to the orthodoxy of the Nicene Creed. The text we sing today has evolved from Ambrose's Latin through Luther's faithful German to several generations of English usage, with some stanzas sometimes dropped along the way. But the basic thrust survives, often in exact phrases. In the opening two stanzas (setting aside a prologue using the opening of Psalm 80, but of disputed authenticity), the exalted references to the Virgin and God's chosen birth echo scripture. Not by human flesh (seed) alone was "the Word of God made flesh" (John 1:14), but by the Breath (Spirit) of God. "The fruit of woman, blossom fresh" recalls Elizabeth's words to Mary about the "fruit of your womb" (Luke 1:42).

Ambrose narrates the incarnation as a rescue mission, in Nicene terms. "Very God and Mary's son, eager now his race to run" (st. 3), Christ both fully divine and human embarks on a journey of God's self-expression down into humanity's plight and back to the height. "From God's heart the Savior speeds, back to God his pathway leads; out to vanquish death's command, back to reign at God's right hand" (st. 4). This *excursus* and *recursus* (Neoplatonic) language of an odyssey has several literary echoes: the circuit course of the sun in Psalm 19:5–6, Homer's Odysseus, Luke's prodigal son, Augustine himself in leaving his mother's church but then returning to it and to her. Beyond all those journeys, the point here is Christ's own rescue mission down into humanity's captivity, even the credal descent into hell, and then back up to the throne. After all, Jesus himself said that he came from the Father into the world and is going back to the Father (John 16:28). Thus, the

Savior of the Nations, Come

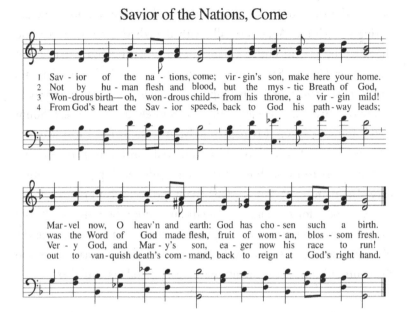

1 Sav - ior of the na - tions, come; vir - gin's son, make here your home.
2 Not by hu - man flesh and blood, but the mys - tic Breath of God,
3 Won-drous birth— oh, won - drous child— from his throne, a vir - gin mild!
4 From God's heart the Sav - ior speeds, back to God his path-way leads;

Mar - vel now, O heav'n and earth: God has cho - sen such a birth.
was the Word of God made flesh, fruit of wom - an, blos - som fresh.
Ver - y God, and Mar - y's son, ea - ger now his race to run!
out to van-quish death's com - mand, back to reign at God's right hand.

5 Now your manger, shining bright,
hallows night with newborn light.
Night cannot this light subdue;
let our faith shine ever new.

6 Praise we sing to Christ the Lord,
virgin's son, incarnate Word!
To the holy Trinity
praise we sing eternally!

Text: attr. Ambrose of Milan, 340-397; Martin Luther, 1483-1546; tr. hymnal version
Music: NUN KOMM, DER HEIDEN HEILAND, J. Walter, *Geistliche Gesangbüchlein*, 1524
Text © 2006 Augsburg Fortress.

incarnation is the saving event, with the light shining in the darkness (st. 5) leading to the trinitarian and anti-Arian doxology in conclusion (st. 6): "Praise we sing to Christ the Lord." In the original stanza 7, Ambrose said that the Son is "equal to the eternal Father," which is explicitly against any Arian subordination of Christ to God the Father.[8]

In general, this hymn and all his others were a crucial part of Ambrose's catechetical ministry, teaching the orthodox Nicene faith.

8   Dunkle, *Ambrose,* 120–129, 216; *One Hundred Latin Hymns, Ambrose to Aquinas,* edited and translated by Peter G. Walsh with Christopher Husch (Cambridge, MA: Harvard University Press, 2012), #5, p. 16. To be cited as Walsh, *Hymns,* and the hymn number (#) and/or the page number.

No wonder that Ambrosian hymnody caught on, stayed in heavy use during the Middle Ages especially with Benedictine daily prayer, and shows up in Martin Luther's translation in the first "Lutheran" hymnals in the 1520s. "Savior of the Nations, Come" in Latin, German, and English (and more) is perhaps the "longest-running" hymn in all of church history.[9] Overall, Ambrose himself deserves every honor as the founder of Christian hymnody, at least in the Latin Western Church, since what he wrote and promoted was not just some poetic texts later set to music but actual congregational singing in his ministry. The naming of "Ambrosian" chant, however, is mostly in honor of his support for singing, since he did not write the music itself. But the good bishop testified to the power of song, and in promoting the Nicene view of Christ as fully divine he created hymns that have stood the course of time across many centuries into today's churches.

Prudentius (348–ca. 410) and "Of the Father's Love Begotten" (ELW 295, LSB 384)

Shortly after Ambrose, another Latin poet also captured the Nicene Creed's basic message in a text that in modern times has become a beloved Christmas hymn: "Of the Father's Love Begotten." Aurelius Prudentius Clemens was a successful lawyer and government official in Spain when he retired to devote his considerable talent in Latin poetry to the Christian cause of honoring the martyrs and connecting daily life to the credal message. Prudentius was apparently in Milan in the late 390s, and his poetry reflects the influence of Bishop Ambrose in several ways. His extensive output, including some hymns for morning prayer, contains occasional references to Christ in Nicene terms as "God from God."[10] One particular passage, noted shortly, clearly champions the Nicene Creed over against the Arian subordination of

---

9   The phrase is Paul Westermeyer's, who is more qualified about it; *ELW Companion* 263. See also the extensive comments in *LSB Companion* 332.

10   See Gerard O'Daly, *Days Linked by Song; Prudentius' Cathemerinon* (Oxford: Oxford University Press, 2012), for introduction and texts, in this case, *Cath.* 6.5–8.

Of the Father's Love Begotten

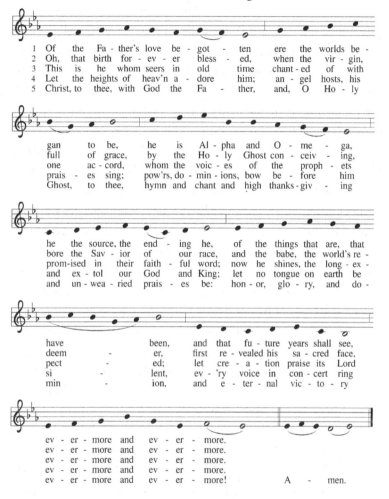

1 Of the Fa - ther's love be - got - ten ere the worlds be -
2 Oh, that birth for - ev - er bless - ed, when the vir - gin,
3 This is he whom seers in old time chant - ed of with
4 Let the heights of heav'n a - dore him; an - gel hosts, his
5 Christ, to thee, with God the Fa - ther, and, O Ho - ly

gan to be, he is Al - pha and O - me - ga,
full of grace, by the Ho - ly Ghost con - ceiv - ing,
one ac - cord, whom the voic - es of the proph - ets
prais - es sing; pow'rs, do - min - ions, bow be - fore him
Ghost, to thee, hymn and chant and high thanks - giv - ing

he the source, the end - ing he, of the things that are, that
bore the Sav - ior of our race, and the babe, the world's re -
prom-ised in their faith - ful word; now he shines, the long - ex -
and ex - tol our God and King; let no tongue on earth be
and un - wea - ried prais - es be: hon - or, glo - ry, and do -

have been, and that fu - ture years shall see,
deem - er, first re - vealed his sa - cred face,
pect - ed; let cre - a - tion praise its Lord
si - lent, ev - 'ry voice in con - cert ring
min - ion, and e - ter - nal vic - to - ry

ev - er - more and ev - er - more.
ev - er - more and ev - er - more.
ev - er - more and ev - er - more.
ev - er - more and ev - er - more.
ev - er - more and ev - er - more! A - men.

Text: Marcus Aurelius Clemens Prudentius, 348–413; tr. composite
Music: DIVINUM MYSTERIUM, plainsong mode V, 13th cent.

Christ as less than fully God. Various parts of Prudentius's poetic corpus filtered into the Christian liturgy over the centuries, but this praise for God the Son is the best known today.

Certain lines from the *Cathemerinon*, Poem 9, were chosen for translation into English by John Mason Neale, who rendered many such ancient texts for his Anglican communion in the nineteenth century and for posterity.[11] The resulting text is also known by its first Latin line, *Corde natus ex parentis*, "Born from the heart of the parent." That Christ was "begotten," not made, fits the Nicene Creed, just as the rest of the first stanza holds, with Christ's own words in Revelation 1, that he is the Alpha or source of all things, "ere the worlds began to be." The Son or Word is in on the creating, not the first creature as Arius was thought to teach. Some modern hymnals then skip the stanza that makes this point by way of Psalm 33:9 or Psalm 148:5 and John 1: "By his Word was all created; he commanded; it was done."[12] The birth forever blessed of the savior and redeemer of the world (st. 2), foretold by poets and prophets (st. 3), is praised in echoes of the Psalms (st. 4). Prudentius went on to many stanzas about Christ's miracles and saving deeds, but closes as the Psalter does with universal praise (*Cath* 9.106–11, Psalms 148–50). Neale added the final "evermore and evermore" to each stanza, and made the concluding doxology explicitly Trinitarian in the Nicene way, as in the *Gloria patri*, but in general he conveyed the chosen portions of Prudentius accurately and memorably.

One more early Nicene poet shows up in later hymnody, both the Roman Catholic morning and evening prayer and also Martin Luther's translations into German. Coelius Sedulius wrote long poems in the fifth century, though little further is known about him; one of them, spanning the life of Christ from A to Z, the incarnation through Christ's miracles to the passion, yielded two hymns. From the start of *A solis ortus* (Psalm 113:3) comes "From East to West" (LSB 385). In Luther's version it is "Jesus We Now Must Laud and Sing" (LW 53:237–39). The middle group of the twenty-three stanzas provides

---

11   For more about Neale, see Paul Westermeyer's comments in the *ELW Companion* regarding ELW 257, and his *Te Deum: The Church and Music* (Minneapolis: Fortress Press, 1998), 274–280. To be cited as Westermeyer, *Te Deum*.

12   Erik Routley, *A Panorama of Christian Hymnody*, edited and expanded by Paul A. Richardson (Chicago: GIA Publications, 2005), #155B. To be cited as Routley-Richardson, *Panorama*, by hymn number (#) and/or page number. The stanza, from *Cath. 9.13*, is also in *Glory to God* (Louisville, KY: Westminster John Knox Press, 2013) 108, st. 2.

"Why, impious Herod, shouldst thou fear" (Matthew 2:3), among Luther's translated hymns as "Herod, Why Dreadest Thou a Foe."[13] In this Epiphany hymn, the Magi sound the same anti-Arian note by praising the newborn as God (originally st. 9, here st. 2).

The whole context of this Trinitarian confession by Ambrose, Prudentius, or Sedulius is represented in many later hymns, famously in "Holy, Holy, Holy" (using Revelation 4; ELW 413) to the tune in fact called NICAEA, in the *Te Deum* (ELW 414 covered under medieval hymns below), and in every musical setting of the Creed itself, such as Luther's "We All Believe in One True God" (ELW 411, LSB 953–54). "Of the Father's Love Begotten" may sound like a gentle Christmas tune but in fact the original text was a direct defense of the Nicene truth of Christ's divinity over against the persistent alternative of the Arians. In the Western realm, the controversy lasted long beyond Ambrose and Prudentius. The exiled Arians became successful missionaries along the western borders of the Empire, with some Germanic tribes adopting their version of Christianity and thus continuing the story into the sixth century.

The Legendary St. Patrick and "I Bind Unto Myself Today" (ELW 450, LSB 604)

The early church has a final famous name to cover here. Ireland's St. Patrick spawned legends through the centuries including a legendary hymn. English by birth and in Ireland originally as a captive slave in the fifth century, Patrick became a famous missionary spreading the Christian message and baptizing thousands. Here, too, the legacy of Nicaea and its creed pertains, for Patrick's "Confession" starts with the full divinity of Christ by whom "are made all things, visible and invisible."[14] Irish-Celtic Christianity then flourished via other missionaries

---

13 *Luther's Works, American Edition,* eds. Jaroslav Pelikan and Helmut T. Lehmann vols. 1–55, Christopher Boyd Brown vols. 56–80 (St. Louis: Concordia Publishing House and Philadelphia: Fortress Press, 1955—), 53:302–303. To be abbreviated as LW, in this case LW 53. For a different translation of the hymn, see LSB 399.

14 Patrick's Confession, 4; *Readings,* Coakley and Sterk, 222.

such as Columba and Columbanus, who in the sixth and seventh centuries established singing communities from the Isle of Iona to Scotland and North Umbria, even to France and elsewhere on the continent. At the Synod of Whitby hosted by the abbess Hilda in 664, Celtic traditions gave way to the Roman and Latin ones in the English church, but they never fully disappeared.

One example is the hymn implausibly attributed to St. Patrick, as translated by Ms. Cecil Frances Alexander for a hymnal in the late 1880s, "I Bind Unto Myself Today" (ELW 450). By legend, Patrick composed and sang this "breastplate" hymn to arm himself (Ephesians 6) against various forms of evil. Since it starts by invoking the Triune name in Nicene terms, it is associated today with baptism and indeed calls on Christ's own baptism and saving history at the start. Modern versions drop some stanzas, such as the "binding" power of the heavenly and human ranks (cherubim and seraphim, prophets and apostles, confessors and patriarchs, in the original stanza 3) against the Satanic perils (sins and vice, spells and wizards, in the original stanzas 6–7), but *Evangelical Lutheran Worship* retains the hymn's striking affirmation of the created realm. "I bind unto myself today the virtues of the star-lit heaven, the glorious sun's life-giving ray," the moon, the lightning, "the deep salt sea, around the old eternal rocks" (st. 3). The hymn may be ancient, perhaps seventh century, and its Irish text does name aspects of creation, but it is probably not by Patrick himself—and in the end, it is not a modern form of Celtic creation spirituality but wholly Christ-centered: "Christ be with me, Christ within me, Christ behind me, Christ before me" (st. 4, originally st. 8).[15]

---

15   See LSB 604 and *LSB Companion* 604, note 6. For a full translation, see Routley-Richardson, *Panorama* #320, 290–291. For another paraphrase, see *All Creation Sings, Evangelical Lutheran Worship Supplement* (Minneapolis: Augsburg Fortress, 2020), 1084, "God, be the love . . . O Christ, surround me" by Richard B. Colligan. Also, "Be Thou My Vision" ELW 793 is thought to stem from early medieval Irish texts, perhaps the eighth century.

3

THE EASTERN AND ORTHODOX EARLY CHURCH
(100-800)

"With hymns of victory"

GREEK PHRASES AND texts were sung in the early church and through
the centuries from the New Testament itself, especially in liturgical
chants. The mentioned *Kyrie eleison* ("Lord, have mercy") is a prime
example. The Greek *Trisagion* ("thrice-holy") builds from Isaiah 6 to
make strong statements about God (holy, mighty, immortal) and to
apply them to Christ too. Singing "Holy God, holy and mighty, holy
and immortal, *crucified for us*" reflected Christological controversies in
the later centuries.[1]

Here, too, fragmentary evidence gives way to a fuller record in
the fourth century. St. Basil (ca. 300–79), the bishop and Nicene theologian known as "the Great," cited a sung text that was familiar and
perhaps already old in his time. The *Phos hilarion* (Joyous or Glad-
some Light) was traditionally sung, perhaps from the third century,
as evening lamps were lit. First translated into English by John Keble
in 1834 at the start of that era's Anglican retrieval of Greek Christian
antiquity, this part of Evening Prayer has been translated and paraphrased many times since. The text is praise for Christ, the true Light.
Evangelical Lutheran Worship provides multiple versions for the "Hymn
of Light" at Vespers (p. 310), such as "Joyous Light of Glory" (ELW
229, from the LBW vespers; see also LSB 888) and Marty Haugen's

---

1   Kimberly Hope Belcher, "Trinitarian Hymns in the East and West," *Hymns and
Hymnody*, vol. 1, 98. See ELW Service Music 159–61 for the original and shorter version.

popular paraphrase and expansion, "Joyous Light of Heavenly Glory" (ELW 561, from "Holden Vespers '86"; see also ELW 230–31, 562–63). Greek liturgical chants developed at great length from the fifth and later centuries as the biblical canticles were augmented with new stanzas (the Canons), although they are rarely known in Western hymn-singing. But there are important exceptions.

Another key fourth-century witness to early Christian worship practices was the pilgrim Egeria, whose narrative to her "sisters" back home, apparently in Spain, describes what we call Holy Week in Jerusalem. As also known from texts by bishops John and Cyril of Jerusalem, these services were highly developed, although the actual texts are not all known. One communion liturgy then was named for the very first bishop of Jerusalem, as traditionally understood, namely, the "Liturgy of St. James," the brother of the Lord. From the fifth century on, the Liturgy of St. John Chrysostom and that of St. Basil added variations to this tradition and are well attested. From this liturgical legacy, the text sung at the processional entrance of the communion bread and wine has become widely known as "Let All Mortal Flesh Keep Silence" (ELW 490 and LSB 621, from Gerard Moultrie's 1864 poem, itself working from John Mason Neale's 1859 prose.)

Called in Greek the *Cherubikon*, named for the cloth bearing the image of the cherubic wings that covered the communion elements, the hymn starts with the prophet Habukkuk's reverent admonition for silence (Habukkuk 2:20). "Fear and trembling" and "full homage" (st. 1) are reinforced by the minor key and stately chant of the tune, although the melody (PICARDY) comes from early modern times. Again, a high Nicene Christology prevails: "Christ our God" (st. 1) and "King of Kings . . . Lord of Lords" (st. 2, from I Timothy 6:15). Even the seraphim and cherubim honor this "Lord Most High" (st. 4) in another echo of Isaiah 6. This is a sacramental reverence of the highest order: "in the body and the blood, he will give to all the faithful his own self for heavenly food" (st. 2). Even as the lay faithful sang and cherished this song, liturgical theologians like

Nicholas Cabasilas centuries later had to point out that at this first entrance of the bread and wine they were not yet the consecrated body and blood of Christ.

Introducing the "early" church meant a straight chronological segue a few pages ago from the accessible biblical literature of the first century CE to the poorly documented second century into the third and then on to the numerous Fathers of the fourth century. But leaving the early church behind is not so straightforward. The Roman Empire changed, in several ways. Constantine not only legalized and then favored Christianity; he also, in 324, moved the capital of the empire from Rome in the Latin West to a "New Rome" in the Greek East, a spot earlier called Byzantium that quickly became known as "Constantine's City" or Constantinople. Under his successor, Theodosius, Nicene Christianity became the state religion and the Arian outlaws were banished.

But Christian unity was elusive, and another controversy over Christ divided the eastern half of the empire into more or less a northeast quadrant of Greeks, who were aligned in this case with the Bishop of Rome, and a southeast quadrant of Egyptians (Copts), with many Syrian Christians too. (We will come back to the Syriac texts, including hymnody, that spread not only east to Iraq, Iran, and even China but also south to Egypt and Ethiopia.) Eastern Christians agreed that the divine Christ was united to human nature, meaning a saving reunion of the divine and the human. But was Christ one person "in two natures," human and divine unmixed and unconfused, as the 451 Council of Chalcedon near Constantinople decreed, or was he one nature (mia-physis) of God incarnate, as the so-called "non-Chalcedonians" in Egypt and parts of Syria asserted before and after 451? The church split, and emperors tried to reunite it, including the great Justinian in the sixth century, but to no avail.

Justinian I (ca. 483–565) is also known for reconquering the parts of the Western Empire that had fallen to the Germanic tribes, but that, too, was not successful for long. His revision of the Roman

Law Code in 529 used Latin as the basic and traditional text, but it thereafter added appendices in Greek. This change of language can symbolize the transition from Latin Rome to a Byzantine (Greek) empire even though these Greek-speaking Christians still called themselves Romans. Soon after Justinian, the empire was reduced to "East Rome" and had less and less to do with the Latin lands.

In the seventh century, Islam took military and political control of great swaths of land and sea, including the southern part of the old empire that was in religious dissent from Constantinople over Chalcedonian Christology. The Mediterranean was now three worlds: the fluid patchwork of Germanic tribes and Roman customs in the (north) west, the Islamic Umayyad dynasty from Spain across North Africa to Egypt and the "Holy Land" with its overall capital in Damascus, and the Greek Byzantine Empire. We will come back to the West shortly, including the odd terminology of "medieval," but first the story of one prolific author touches on both the Byzantine Christian Empire and the Umayyad Islamic realm.

John of Damascus (ca. 670–ca. 750)

John of Damascus

Two standard Easter hymns can lead us to a poet who is better known for his doctrinal summaries, his defense of icons, and his critique of Islam: namely, John of Damascus. Even without exact years for his birth or death, John's life span roughly coincides with another momentous era (675–750), when Islam made its capital in Damascus under the Umayyad dynasty, before its move to Baghdad with the Abbasid dynasty. Contrary to Hollywood myths, Christians in Damascus and throughout the Islamic realm were not all immediately wiped out but often lived on, albeit under the major restrictions in the "Pact of Omar" regarding taxation and public life. In fact, John was quite involved in all this in Damascus since his father (and grandfather) had been the official representatives of the city's Chalcedonian Christians to the Islamic caliph regarding such restrictions and the payment of the taxes. Later in life, John left this context, perhaps including his own service in that post, and apparently served as a priest in Jerusalem and perhaps even as an aide to the Patriarch there (705–737?). Then he retreated into monastic life for prayer, study, and writing, all to great effect. His summary of *The Orthodox Faith* provided an influential distillation of the Greek Fathers, from the Nicene era through subsequent councils and centuries of disputed doctrines. Attached to it was an account of the many related heresies, culminating in his critique of Muslim beliefs and thereby giving posterity the earliest theological analysis of Islam.

There were a few earlier comments about Muslims by other Christian authors, but John's account was more thorough, and much more influential later on. He treated the Islamic view of Christ not as another religion but as a heresy, again like the Arians because they subordinated Christ to a lesser role. John thereby defended the Christian view of God as triune, that God's Word and God's Spirit, both mentioned in the Koran, really were God and were not to be cut off from God as the Muslim "mutilators" thought. Since Islam had also claimed that there could be no visual images of this transcendent God, a position that some Christian theologians have shared, John also wrote a careful defense of icons, especially images of Christ. The success of his

arguments for icons had great influence upon the course of Byzantine church life.[2] On all three fronts (summarizing Christian theology,
opposing heresies including Islam, in his view, and defending icons),
John's writings were enormously important in this transitional age
even beyond the poetic works traditionally associated with him and
known today as Easter hymns. Like Ambrose in the early Latin church
and some later Latin theologians, especially Bernard of Clairvaux and
Thomas Aquinas (not to mention Martin Luther), John's fame is first
of all for his portfolio of theological writings in general, shaping an
entire era, and only secondarily for our topic of hymn texts.

"The Day of Resurrection!" (ELW 361, LSB 478) "Come, You Faithful, Raise the Strain" (ELW 363, LSB 487)

John's overall theological emphasis on Christ as God incarnate and
risen also serves to anchor his poetic or hymnic output. Attributed to
him are specific "canons," building on the biblical canticles mentioned
earlier, in this case the triumphant Song of Moses/Miriam (Exodus
15) as pertains to the Easter season.[3] These are hymns of victory. John's
Easter canon, the source of "The Day of Resurrection," became so
widely used in the Orthodox Church, to the present, that he has been
generously but mistakenly credited with many more examples of litur-
gical/sung poetry, much as Ambrose and Pope Gregory I (Saint Gregory the Great) became credited with Ambrosian or Gregorian chants
that they never wrote. John may have written canons on the Transfiguration and on the Dormition (Falling Asleep) of Mary. For Morning
Prayer early on Easter Day itself, John's Easter canon, called the Paschal
Canon and later the "Queen of Canons," makes the most of the Pasch

---

2   For a recent summary, see Anna Chrysostomides, "John of Damascus' Theology
of Icons in the Context of Eighth-Century Palestinian Iconoclasm," *Dumbarton Oaks
Papers* 75 (2021), 263–295.

3   For more on "canons" and related types of Byzantine music, see Dimitrios
Skrekas, "Byzantine Song in the Early Centuries, From Kantakion to the Canon,"
Hymns and Hymnody, vol. 1, 64–80.

or "Passover," not the ritual but the crossing over the Red Sea. In the first part or ode of the canon, "The Day of Resurrection," John quotes an Easter sermon by one of the Greek Fathers he elsewhere summarized so thoroughly, namely, the fourth-century Gregory Nazianzen or Gregory the Theologian, who was also a poet.[4]

"The day of resurrection! Earth, tell it out abroad, the passover of gladness, the passover of God. From death to life eternal, from sin's dominion free [literally, 'from earth to heaven'], our Christ has brought us over, with hymns of victory" (ELW 361, st. 1). The *Evangelical Lutheran Worship* version supplies only the first three stanzas of John Mason Neale's translation and then adds a doxology.

For the second Sunday of Easter, John's other well-known canon starts with "Come, You Faithful," which again echoes Miriam's canticle: "led them with unmoistened foot through the Red Sea waters" (st. 1). The second and third stanzas attach the resurrection to the northern hemisphere's passage of seasons from winter to spring. Then it goes on to allude to Christ's appearance(s) to the disciples, befitting "Doubting Thomas" Sunday. The original Greek makes explicit that the greeting of "peace" in stanza 4 is to "his friends" as in John 20. "Neither could the gates of death, nor the tomb's dark portal, nor the watchers, not the seal, hold you as a mortal; but today, among your own [friends], you appear, bestowing your deep peace which evermore passes human knowing" (ELW 363, st. 4). As we saw with the Latin "Of the Father's Love Begotten," it was John Mason Neale who translated John's canons, indeed the full texts not just these small portions, from Greek into English as part of his major Anglican retrieval of Greek Christian antiquity. Hymnals have been using Neale's effective translations ever since, albeit with many stanzas dropped out.

---

4   Oration 1,1; see Andrew Louth, *St. John Damascene, Tradition and Originality in Byzantine Theology* (Oxford: Oxford University Press, 2002), 258–259, plus his book on John forthcoming from Lexington/Fortress Academic. For Gregory and "O Light that knew no dawn," see Routley-Richardson, *Panorama*, #184.

The Day of Resurrection!

1 The day of res - ur - rec - tion! Earth, tell it out a - broad,
2 Let hearts be purged of e - vil that we may see a - right
3 Now let the heav'ns be joy - ful, let earth its song be - gin,
4 All praise to God the Fa - ther, all praise to Christ the Son,

the pass - o - ver of glad - ness, the pass - o - ver of God.
the Lord in rays e - ter - nal of res - ur - rec - tion light,
the round world keep high tri - umph and all that is there - in.
all praise to God the Spir - it, e - ter - nal Three in One!

From death to life e - ter - nal, from sin's do - min - ion free,
and lis - t'ning to his ac - cents, may hear, so calm and plain,
Let all things, seen and un - seen, their notes of glad - ness blend;
Let all the ran - somed num - ber fall down be - fore the throne,

our Christ has brought us o - ver with hymns of vic - to - ry.
his own "All hail!" and hear - ing, may raise the glad re - frain.
for Christ the Lord has ris - en, our joy that has no end!
and hon - or, pow'r, and glo - ry as - cribe to God a - lone!

Text: John of Damascus, c. 696–c. 754; tr. John Mason Neale, 1818–1866, alt.
Music: ELLACOMBE, German melody, 18th cent.; adapt. X. L. Hartig, *Melodien zum Mainzer Gesangbuche*, 1833

John of Damascus thus represents an enormous legacy of theological literature in general and hymns in particular. His overall importance even transcends the Greek traditions glimpsed here,

Come, You Faithful, Raise the Strain

1 Come, you faith - ful, raise the strain of tri - um - phant glad - ness!
2 'Tis the spring of souls to - day: Christ has burst his pris - on,
3 Now the queen of sea - sons, bright with the day of splen - dor,
4 Nei - ther could the gates of death, nor the tomb's dark por - tal,
5 Al - le - lu - ia! now we cry to our Lord im - mor - tal,

God has brought forth Is - ra - el in - to joy from sad - ness,
and from three days' sleep in death as a sun has ris - en.
with the roy - al feast of feasts comes its joy to ren - der;
nor the watch - ers, nor the seal, hold you as a mor - tal:
who tri - um - phant burst the bars of the tomb's dark por - tal;

loosed from Pha - raoh's bit - ter yoke Ja - cob's sons and daugh - ters;
All the win - ter of our sins, long and dark, is fly - ing
comes to glad Jer - u - sa - lem, who with true af - fec - tion
but to - day, a - mong your own, you ap - pear, be - stow - ing
Al - le - lu - ia! with the Son God the Fa - ther prais - ing;

led them with un - moist - ened foot through the Red Sea wa - ters.
from the Light to whom we give laud and praise un - dy - ing.
wel - comes in un - wea - ried strain Je - sus' res - ur - rec - tion!
your deep peace, which ev - er - more pass - es hu - man know - ing.
Al - le - lu - ia! yet a - gain to the Spir - it rais - ing.

Text: John of Damascus, c. 696–c. 754; tr. John Mason Neale, 1818–1866, alt.
Music: GAUDEAMUS PARITER, Johann Horn, 1490–1547

because his *Orthodox Faith* was translated into Latin in time to influence medieval scholastic theologians such as Thomas Aquinas. With a reach across so many topics, and even across the growing divide between Byzantium and the Latin writers in the western Middle Ages, the Damascene is one of the most influential theologians in all of Christian history.

Unfortunately, other parts of the Orthodox history of church singing are not as well known in the West as John's contribution. For one example, the sixth-century Romanos the Melodist, a Syrian living in Constantinople, is famed even in his name for the melodic creativity of his poetry and drama, but none of it appears in western hymnals. After John, among other Greek liturgical poets, the nun Kassia in the ninth century also deserves fuller attention especially for her powerful Holy Week hymn about the penitent and tearful Mary Magdalene, "the woman fallen into many sins."[5]

Syriac Poetry to the East and South, Including Ethiopia

Ephrem the Syrian

Although the hymns known today from the Eastern Orthodox side of the early church come mostly from Greek authors such as John of Damascus, there is another large group of Eastern or Oriental Churches whose hymn writers used and still use another language altogether: Syriac. As linked to Aramaic, the tongue of Jesus himself, Syriac has had a long and prestigious literary tradition, especially in

---

5   Egon Wellesz, *A History of Byzantine Music and Hymnography,* 2nd ed. (Oxford: Clarendon, 1998), 395–397. For more on Kassia, the only woman whose hymns have been admitted into the liturgy of the Orthodox Church, see Kurt Sherry, *Kassia the Nun in Context: The Religious Thought of a Ninth-Century Byzantine Monastic* (Piscataway, NJ: Gorgias Press, 2013).

hymnody. The leading figure here is Ephrem the Syrian (ca. 306–73), historically the most prolific and important hymn writer who is missing from hymnals today. His career, in Nisibis on the shifting border between the Roman and Persian empires and then in Edessa at the end of his life, led to fame not only among Syrians, Greeks, and Latins, but also in Coptic, Armenian, Georgian, Ethiopian, and even Arabic Christian legacies.

Deacon Ephrem's voluminous poetry, written explicitly to be sung by church choirs of women, among others, emphasized Christ's incarnation and thus Mary's womb as well as sacramental symbolism and some ethical issues. From his Hymns on the Nativity, twenty-eight of them in a widely available collection, the miraculous paradox of the incarnation receives multiple expressions.

> Mary bore a mute Babe though in Him were hidden all our tongues.
> Joseph carried Him, yet hidden in Him was a silent nature older than everything.
> The Lofty One became like a little child, yet hidden in Him was a treasure of Wisdom that suffices for all.
> He was lofty but he sucked Mary's milk, and from His blessings all creation sucks.
> He is the Living Breast of living breath; by His life the dead were suckled, and they revived.[6]

After Ephrem, the larger story of Syriac-speaking Christians is complicated by doctrinal disputes and the resulting departures from the Roman Empire. Just as the fourth-century conciliar verdicts on Nicene

---

6   "Hymn on the Nativity 4," lines 146–150, *Ephrem the Syrian: Hymns,* translated and introduced by Kathleen E. McVey (New York: Paulist Press, 1989), 100. For more on Ephrem, see McVey's introduction as well as Tala Jarjour, "Syriac Song in the Early Centuries," in *Hymns and Hymnody,* vol. 1, 36–48.

truth and the error of Arius led to the exile of the latter's followers out of the empire to the northwest, so the next century's condemnation of a different heresy in 431 meant another departure of the losing side, this time to the east. Those who sympathized with Nestorius, once bishop of Constantinople, left the empire and moved through Syria to join Christians already in the old Persian realm of today's Iraq and Iran where they still survive, barely. From Baghdad, the capital of the Umayyad Islamic dynasty where they found themselves in dialogue with Muslims including the caliph, they sent missionaries even further east, to China.

After yet a different fifth-century dispute—namely, the Chalcedonian divide mentioned earlier—some other refugees, considered Syrians and called the Nine Saints by later Ethiopian tradition, famously fled the empire's decrees, traveling around 500 CE through the large non-Chalcedonian realm of Egypt. The Coptic Orthodox Church has its own long history including liturgical song, as centered in Alexandria but stretching its jurisdiction up the Nile as far as Ethiopia. The Nine Saints became famous in the Christian kingdom of Aksum for several reasons. Ethiopia was already officially a Christian nation since the conversion of King Ezana in the mid-fourth century. But these sainted figures are credited with leading a growth surge in Ethiopian Christianity, from Abba Aragawi as the founder of the famous monastery Debre Damo high on a secluded mesa, through others with their own accomplishments, to Abba Garima who penned the first translation of the New Testament into Ethiopic, the Garima Gospels still extant today. Alongside the Nine Saints, according to Ethiopian tradition, was Yared, a priest from Aksum called "the melodious" for his "invention of Ethiopian sacred music and hymnody," also unknown in western hymnals.[7] In general, the legendary Nine Saints from Syria advised the powerful Christian

7   Antonella Brita, "Yared," *Encyclopaedia Aethiopica*, vol. 5, ed. Alessandro Bausi (Wiesbaden: Harrassowitz, 2014), 26.

Yared of Aksum (Ethiopia)

kings, spread the faith far beyond Aksum, and advanced this African church through the sixth century, long before most of northern Europe was Christian at all.

However, for all its Syriac antiquity and poetic power, the liturgical music of this entire tradition, including the Ethiopians, has not led to congregational hymnody well-known in the West. Yet see "Strengthen for Service, Lord" (ELW 497), from the Syriac liturgy of Malabar in India, for a glimpse of its symbolic range, invoking hands, ears, tongues, eyes, and feet to express the faith.

Summary

To sum up the "early church" hymnody of these two chapters, the Latin side featured poems and congregational hymns that helped combat the tenacious Arian heresy of subordinating Christ as not fully divine. The Greek side of the story gave us texts that were originally sung in the flow of the Orthodox liturgy and have, over time, become hymns in many other churches. Just as hymns by John of Damascus have crossed centuries, languages, and confessional boundaries, so did other examples within the early church. Ambrose of Milan learned from the Greeks, and Egeria and Cassian brought Eastern customs to the West. So too the Syriac literature including poetry was carried across many boundaries, east to Baghdad and beyond as well as south to Alexandria in Egypt and Axum in Ethiopia.

The western and eastern areas of the old Roman Empire were also bound together early on by the Nicene Creed, whether in Latin or in Greek, especially about Christ as fully God. But soon, when the Roman Empire divided, they would differ on the Holy Spirit, as also evident in medieval hymnody.

⚜ 4 ⚜

THE "DARK" AGES?

The Early Middle Ages (500–1100)

Te Deum: *"We Praise You, O God"*

PROTESTANTS SING MORE hymns from the Middle Ages than they might realize, including several from early in the so-called "Dark" Ages. Palm Sunday often begins with an early medieval processional, "All Glory, Laud, and Honor," and Holy Week can culminate with "O Sacred Head, Now Wounded." Plus, *Do, re, mi* turns out to be a Latin music lesson from a medieval teacher.

Parallel to "primeval" for "first era," the word "medieval" means "middle era" and is thus the equivalent of "Middle Ages." But, middle of what? Naming a group of centuries in that retrospective way stems from some Italian humanists in the fifteenth century. Flavio Biondo set 410–1400 as a "middle," and Leonardo Bruni in 1442 called 476–1250 a "middle" period.[1] If their own time was a Renaissance (rebirth), as later historians codified it, then the framing of history became tripartite: their own time of revival, the classical antiquity that was being reborn, and thus some pejorative gap, even "Dark" Ages, in the middle; hence, medieval. The Renaissance, in other words, concocted some "middle" era in order to identify itself by way of contrast.

---

1   On the idea of naming an era "middle," see Anthony Grafton, "Middle Ages," *The Dictionary of the Middle Ages* (New York: Charles Scribner's Sons, 1987), 8: 308–309.

But the nomenclature from these later western Europeans does not fit the Byzantine or Islamic realms or the rest of the world. The starting points for Biondo and Bruni were taken from what they thought were decisive western events representing the fall of the Roman Empire. In 410, the heart of the Roman Empire was invaded by Attila's Huns and in 476 the last (western) Roman Emperor stepped down. From the fifth to the fifteenth centuries is a long haul, with many hymns to cover. By tradition we speak of the plural Middle Ages, with chapters here on what has been called the "Dark" Ages (500–1100), then the (High) Middle Ages (1100–1300), and finally the "late" medieval era (1300–1500), here also called "Reforms before the Reformation." Perhaps the sheer quantity of medieval texts that are still sung today will surprise those who think that hymns were really a Protestant invention.

The sixth century (500–600) serves as a period of transition from antiquity to the early Middle Ages in Western Europe, including the decline of the Roman Empire there. These early medieval centuries may sometimes have been called the "Dark Ages," but there are many luminous hymn texts to testify otherwise. The mixture of Roman customs with the migrating peoples (the Goths, Huns, Vandals, sometimes called the Germanic tribes) varied dramatically by place and even by decade, but the representative story of one "barbarian" queen turned Christian nun can introduce a highly educated hymn writer of note.

Radegund and the Hymns of Fortunatus (Sixth Century)

The life of Radegund (ca. 518–87), queen and saint, spans the tumultuous sixth century and can represent the volatile mixture of warring Germanic-Frankish tribes and the Christian culture on the borderlands of the western Roman Empire. Born to Thuringian royalty, she became a captive child bride for the conquering Franks who were adopting Christianity and other Roman ways. She was forced to marry King Clothar, son of Clotilde and Clovis. Queen Clotilde had helped persuade her husband Clovis to be baptized around 500 as a Nicene

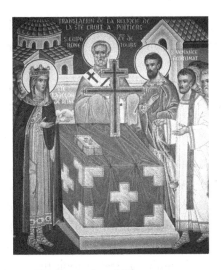

Radegund and Fortunatus

Christian, not an Arian, and this king's name became key to French royal history when spelled as Louis (the First). Radegund was given a Christian education and took it so seriously that she left her brutal husband for the ascetic and monastic life of discipline and prayer. In mid-life at mid-century Radegund used Caesarius's *Rule of Arles* to start a convent in Poitiers, not as the abbess but nevertheless providing queenly and financial leadership. One famous example of her influence leads us to some enduring hymnody and the illustrious career of its author. In 569 Radegund's wealth and royal connections secured from the Byzantine Empire a piece of the True Cross, a precious relic calling for a triumphant processional arrival in Poitiers with poetry suitable to the occasion.

Enter Venantius Fortunatus, the prolific Roman poet who later authored the queen's dramatic life story as well as that of the area's famous Saint, Martin of Tours. Fortunatus (ca. 530—ca. 605) also represents the sixth-century Christian mixture of old and new, the noble Roman traditions and the upstart Frankish aspirations. His voluminous literary output applied a classical Latin education, having learned Virgil and Horace at Ravenna, to epitaphs and narratives for the royal and ecclesial dignitaries in Gallic lands, especially around Poitiers. To welcome the relic, Radegund turned to this classical poet, someone she knew well from his visits to her community and from his various writings, both formal and casual. The result was a long poem containing the "Holy Cross" hymns, found partially in some hymnals today as "The Royal Banners Forward Go" (LBW 124, LSB 455).

Fortunatus wrote very compressed and complex poems, and this one "has defeated every known translator so far," according to Erik Routley.[2] Rather than quote a paraphrase such as John Mason Neale's influential attempt, a prose approximation of the opening verse can convey the power attributed to the cross itself, so welcome in Poitiers that Radegund's community thereafter took the name Monastery of the Holy Cross. "The banners of the King come forth; brightly gleams the mystery of the Cross, on which Life suffered death, and by His death, obtained for us life."[3] The text goes on to itemize aspects of the crucifixion that are simultaneously signs of Christ's "reign in triumph from the tree."[4] After that first triumphant procession in November of 569, this text has been chanted at Vespers in Holy Week through the centuries.

Another hymn by Fortunatus shares this theme and as a marching song may also have been part of the same processional. *Pange, lingua*, in ten stanzas, was also loosely translated by John Mason Neale, then truncated and with further adjustments. "Sing, my tongue, the glorious battle; tell the triumph far and wide; tell aloud the wondrous story of the cross, the Crucified; tell how Christ, the world's redeemer,

2   Routley-Richardson, *Panorama*, p. 120.
3   *The Hymns of the Breviary and Missal*, rev. ed. Matthew Britt OSB (New York: Benzinger Brothers, 1924), 124.
4   *Lutheran Book of Worship* (Minneapolis: Augsburg Publishing House, 1978), 124, st. 3; to be cited as LBW. See also LSB 455, st. 3. As to the Septuagint (Greek) version of Psalm 96:10 referring to a tree, which Christians applied to the cross, see Walsh, *Hymns*, p. 424.

vanquished death the day he died" (ELW 355, st.1; LSB 454; also LBW 118). At times poetically addressed directly *to* the "tree of glory" (st. 5), to the "faithful cross" (st. 6), this text fits the original adoration of the relic of the True Cross as well as annual Holy Week services in many contexts.[5]

Venantius Fortunatus also wrote some lines for an Easter service, lines that have been often adapted for several other festivals: "Hail Thee, Festival Day" (ELW 394, LSB 489). For Easter around 570, he composed a long poem for Bishop Felix of Nantes, celebrating the resurrection of course but also the bishop's triumph in bringing a group of Saxons to the baptismal font. Again, this volatile era of Germanic tribes converting to Christianity, sometimes by force, peeks through the poet's play on their name as a rocky "hard race, the Saxons, living like wild animals."[6] As a whole, the poem spends a long time on the glories of spring and then connects nature's splendor to Easter. The hymn text today is a cut and paste of various lines, plus later additions. Stanza 1 of the hymn ("All the fair beauty of earth from the death of winter arising! Every good gift of the year now with its master [Lord] returns," from lines 31–32) precedes the famous refrain: "Hail thee, festival day! Blest day to be hallowed forever; day when our Lord was raised, breaking the kingdom of death" (lines 39–40). The second stanza combines lines 33–34 and 37–38 in loose paraphrase. Over time, other and alternative stanzas were added, some from medieval English contexts, for the festivals of the Ascension and Pentecost.[7] In

---

5   Fortunatus also inspired Thomas Aquinas in the thirteenth century, as we shall see, to write his own *Pange, lingua*: "Of the glorious body telling, o my tongue, its myst'ries sing" (LBW 120). See also Fortunatus, *Crux benedicta nitet*, Walsh, *Hymns*, #22, and a Swedish version sometimes in English as "Praise the Savior Now and Ever" (LBW 155).

6   The poem, in this case *Carm* 3.9, line 103, is cited and discussed at some length in Michael Robert, *The Humblest Sparrow: The Poetry of Venantius Fortunatus* (Ann Arbor: University of Michigan Press, 2009), 139–164.

7   See *LSB Companion* 489 for more detail.

its current form, part of the appeal comes from Ralph Vaughan Williams's rousing refrain and challenging melodies for the stanzas.

The writings of Venantius Fortunatus go far beyond these hymn texts, culminating in his glowing hagiographies of Radegund and Saint Martin of Tours under the patronage of Bishop (and Saint) Gregory of Tours. Late in his life Fortunatus himself became the bishop of Poitiers and was venerated eventually as a saint.

Benedictine Song

The sixth century has one more transitional development that is crucial to medieval church history in general and to church song in particular: Benedict's *Rule*, as championed by Pope Gregory I around 600. The dominance of the Benedictine Order of medieval monks and nuns leads to many important topics, and for our story especially to their striking discipline of singing through all one hundred and fifty Psalms every week. The *Rule* of St. Benedict (RB), traditionally dated to 529 CE, carefully spreads the Psalter out over the seven daily offices (such as Morning Prayer and Vespers) for the days of the week. It allows that the specifics could vary *as long as* all the Psalms are sung each and every week (RB 18). The text frequently and casually mentions that the *Gloria Patri* (Glory to the Father . . .) should be sung after the Psalms and other readings, in "honor and reverence for the Holy Trinity" (RB 9). This addition, widely practiced for centuries, makes not merely a Christian claim on Israel's texts but also a specifically Nicene and anti-Arian one. The *Rule* also specified other texts to be sung, such as the *Te Deum,* and for the daily hours some unspecified "Ambrosian hymns" (RB 11–13, 17; RB 18).

At the time there were other monastic houses and rules, such as the *Rule of Arles* adopted by Radegund's community, which also named some hymns for the hours of the day. But the Benedictine variety soon dominated the field of medieval monasticism, in great part because of the advocacy of Pope Gregory I. Gregory ruled, with great and long-lasting influence on the Latin church and European society, from 590 to 604. From his reign and profound writings he is called "the Great," quite apart from legends about Gregorian chant. Living as a Benedictine himself, Gregory wrote up the stories of Benedict's legendary life, and championed the use of his *Rule* not only in Rome but also on the mission fields he created, such as England. The Benedictine dominance of western monasticism was sealed when Charlemagne's son made it the only order to be allowed in the Carolingian Empire in the early ninth century. Thus, the medieval monastics, men and women singing the Psalms throughout the day every day, were all various types of Benedictines for centuries, until Francis of Assisi was allowed to start a different sort of order in the thirteenth century. Their pattern of sung prayer influenced medieval worship life generally, including the texts to be sung and how to sing them, and gradually even to the parish level of the Sunday Mass.

Bright Hymns from the "Dark" Ages; the *Te Deum* (ELW 228, LSB 223–25 and LSB 939–41)

The early Middle Ages, the sixth through the eleventh century (500–1100), is the period sometimes labeled the "Dark Ages," as mentioned, but for the wrong reason. As seen already in Fortunatus and the Benedictines, the era was not all darkness and ignorance. It is true that only a minority of the population in early medieval Europe was able to read and write, but that has been true of most cultures in most premodern centuries. There were various enlightened authors to admire in these centuries, such as Dhuoda, the mother whose book advising her son began with a Latin acrostic so subtle that it remained undetected for centuries, or Eriugena, the profound Irish theologian who combined the Greek Fathers with the Augustinian tradition.[8] But for some long stretches, as in the very early church, there is so little textual evidence that we remain in the dark about many aspects of early

---

8   On Dhuoda and other well-educated early medieval women, see my article "The Company of Medieval Women Theologians," *Theology Today* 60.1 (2003), 84–85.

medieval life. There are some excellent, highly literate hymn texts, but they are of uncertain authorship and dates. Between Fortunatus and the twelfth-century historical detail about Bernard of Clairvaux and others, we know little about the origins of some wonderful and famous hymns. The texts may be luminous, but we are the ones in the dark about their origins.

The greatest of the early medieval anonymous hymns is the *Te Deum*, "We Praise You, O God." Mentioned in both Benedict's *Rule* (RB 11) and the *Rule of Arles* in the sixth century, it was by then already a standard feature of monastic singing. And yet it was anonymous. In the ninth century a charming legend emerged that when St. Ambrose baptized St. Augustine at the Easter vigil back in 387, they spontaneously created the *Te Deum* in proper Ambrosian antiphonal style, alternating the verses between them from beginning to end. By then the *Te Deum* had become so wide in usage and high in importance, almost like a creed, such that a miraculous duet by the two sainted Latin Church Fathers seemed an appropriate origin story. Modern attempts to claim a more mundane human authorship, such as by one Nicetas, have never achieved consensus. Perhaps anonymity is in fact more appropriate. The *Te Deum*, in its biblical and credal contents, its universal coverage of heaven and earth, its sheer force of praise for God, is more than another hymn. The full text should be appreciated.[9]

Te Deum: We Praise You, O God

1   *We praise you, O God, we acclaim you as Lord;*
    all creation worships you, the Father everlasting.

2   *To you all angels, all the pow'rs of heav'n,*
    the cherubim and seraphim, sing in endless praise:

---

9   ELW 228; see also LSB 223–25 and 939–41.

3 *Holy, holy, holy Lord, God of pow'r and might,*
heaven and earth are full of your glory.

4 *The glorious company of apostles praise you.*
The noble fellowship of prophets praise you.

5 *The white-robed army of martyrs praise you.*
Throughout the world the holy church acclaims you:

6 *Father, of majesty unbounded; your true and only*
Son, worthy of all praise;
the Holy Spirit, advocate and guide.

7 *You, Christ, are the king of glory,*
the eternal Son of the Father.

8 *When you took our flesh to set us free*
you humbly chose the Virgin's womb.

9 *You overcame the sting of death*
and opened the kingdom of heaven to all believers.

10 *You are seated*
at God's right hand in glory.

11 *We believe that you will come*
to be our judge.

12 *Come, then, Lord, and help your people,*
bought with the price of your own blood,

13 *and bring us with your saints*
to glory everlasting.

[Stanzas 14–17 are not part of the original canticle but have often been appended.]

14   *Save your people, Lord, and bless your inheritance.*
   Govern and uphold them now and always.

15   *Day by day we bless you.*
   We praise your name forever.

16   *Keep us today, Lord, from all sin.*
   Have mercy on us, Lord, have mercy.

17   *Lord, show us your love and mercy, for we have*
   put our trust in you. In you, Lord, is our hope: let
   us never be put to shame.

The first word, "You," keeps the emphasis on God, triune and especially in Christ, and many lines repeat that verbal starting point. In stanza 3, the biblical foundation (from Isaiah 6 and Revelation 4) echoes the *Sanctus* in the Mass, and the concluding lines are all from the Psalms. God is praised from the angelic heights of heaven and from the roll call of human history. The trinitarian stanza 6 leads to the explicitly Nicene and Ambrosian affirmation of the "eternal" Son of the Father in stanza 7, something no Arian could sing. The very center of the *Te Deum* is the incarnation and triumph of Christ in stanzas 8–9. After the praise and confession of faith comes also the cry for help in stanzas 12 and beyond, supplemented by additional petitions straight from the Psalms.

From its emergence in the early Middle Ages, the *Te Deum* became a liturgical and musical centerpiece in Christian ceremonies of all kinds. From regular Saturday evening prayer for all Benedictines, it rose to exalted rites such as installations of bishops and coronations of kings. Martin Luther praised it like a creed and rendered it into German (see LW 53: 171–75), but modern hymnals more often adapt the German version that appeared in a 1774 Roman Catholic hymnal by Father Ignaz Franz, translated by Clarence A. Walworth as "Holy God, We Praise Your Name" (ELW 414 and LSB 940). That hymn version retains the strong note of praise and the broad scope from angels to prophets and martyrs, but the shortened form that is used most often drops the credal focus on Christ at the center. Over time, the *Te Deum* has gone beyond church use to special concert versions by famous composers such as Haydn, Mozart, and Verdi, even appearing prominently early in Puccini's opera *Tosca*. A military band played the tune from the 1774 German hymnal version when Angela Merkel concluded her service as Germany's Chancellor in 2021. Perhaps its anonymity suits all this attention, transcending any specific authorial context; in any case, the text itself stands as a bright witness against the dim reputation of the "Dark" Ages.[10]

There are other anonymous hymns from the early Middle Ages (500–1100) that are commonly sung today. Although we do not know the individual authors, and thus the specific contexts, the texts nevertheless reveal some general patterns of historical interest. As with the *Te Deum*, these texts can add further evidence against the stereotype of a benighted era.

"That Easter Day with Joy Was Bright" (ELW 384) is a small portion of a hymn, perhaps sixth century, that juxtaposes the daily rising of the sun with the unique rising of the "sun of righteousness" (Malachi 4:2), the Son of God. It was apparently one of the early morning hymns for the monastic daily office, as Benedict's *Rule* had recommended. Hymns for dawn, mid-morning (the "third" or "sixth" hours), afternoon, evening, and midnight were sung often and collected into what has been called the "Old Hymnal."[11]

---

10   LSB 939–41, with documentation in *LSB Companion*. For general information, see Carl P. E. Springer, "Reflections on Lutheran Worship, Classics, and the *Te Deum*," *Logia* 5.4 (1996): 31–43.

11   Walsh, *Hymns*, xi, #23–35.

"Christ Is Made the Sure Foundation" (ELW 645, LSB 909 and 912) is the second half of a seventh or eighth century hymn about the blessed heavenly Jerusalem. The half in modern hymnals deftly applies the biblical language for Christ as cornerstone (Ephesians 2 and I Peter 2, citing Psalm 118:22, Isaiah 28:16, and Matthew 21:42) to several features of a building, such as foundation and walls, and has been used accordingly for church dedications. A stanza missing from major Lutheran hymnals specifies that this is a singing church: "All that dedicated city, dearly loved by God on high, in exultant jubilation pours perpetual melody."[12]

"Creator of the Stars of Night" (eighth century or earlier; ELW 245 and LSB 351) is addressed to Christ the Creator and Redeemer, continuing the anti-Arian theme of Ambrose discussed earlier. The ELW second stanza reflects the biblical reason for connecting an evening hymn to the season of Advent: "when this old world drew on toward night [Hebrews 9:26], you came; but not in splendor bright." The third stanza paraphrases Philippians 2, and the fourth (originally sixth) inserted the Greek word for holy (*Hagios*) into the Latin text.[13] Biblical literacy and sparking vocabulary again rebut the assumption of ignorance in the early Middle Ages.

There is another linkage in these three examples. These and many more (a dozen in ELW, eighteen in LSB) were translated into English by John Mason Neale, who also spoke glowingly of this "treasury . . . of noble hymns" that had been neglected so long before his labors that we value today.[14]

One more medieval hymn, not of Neale's labors, can confirm the biblical familiarity in the luminous poetry of this age. "Hark, A Thrilling Voice is Sounding" (ELW 246, LSB 345), as translated by Edward Caswall, combines scriptural images in every stanza starting with John the Baptist's cry in Mark 1. In stanza one, darkness and day come from

12   Routley-Richardson, *Panorama* #158B, p. 146.
13   Walsh, *Hymns*, #48, pp. 167 and 445.
14   J. M. Neale, *English Hymnody*, p. 303; cited in *Hymns and Hymnody*, vol. 1, 170.

Romans 13:12. "Christ our sun" in stanza two echoes Malachi 4:2, Isaiah 60, and Revelation 22:16. The Lamb with pardon in stanza three is John the Baptist's proclamation from John 1. Fear and Christ coming again in glory are straight out of Luke 21.26–27. As so often, the hymn ends with the trinitarian doxology.

This pattern of biblically literate, theologically learned early medieval hymnody continues with other examples where the authorship is more or less certain, despite some ambiguities. The Venerable Bede (672–735), famous for his *Ecclesiastical History* of the English people, also wrote biblical expositions and some hymns. A very few survive, such as "A Hymn of Glory Let Us Sing!" (ELW 393). Bede also relates the story of "Caedmon's Hymn," the first known poem in (Old) English.[15]

Carolingian Hymns and the Conflict over the Holy Spirit

Two other early medieval hymns for which we can identify probable authorship have long histories of heavy use in church singing. The context for both features Charlemagne (Charles the Great), the king of the Franks who was crowned emperor by Pope Leo III in 800. Pepin, Charles's father, had previously secured papal approval for his family line to be consecrated as kings. When the Eastern or Byzantine Empire and emperors seemed more and more irrelevant to church and state in Western Europe, it was not surprising that the pope agreed to an imperial coronation on Christmas Day of 800. Charlemagne had already succeeded in military and economic affairs, and was cultivating reforms in educational and cultural realms, especially for monastic communities and clergy. The "Carol" or Karl in Carolingian stands for Charles's leadership of the times, launching the "Holy Roman Empire," an era sometimes even considered a Renaissance of sorts. These two hymns point to different features of that context, but both testify to the high quality of Latin poetry in

---

15 See Bede's *History of the English Church,* 4, 24; *Hymns and Hymnody,* vol. 1, 110.

that day. The second one introduces a theological topic of permanent ecumenical significance.

"All Glory, Laud, and Honor" (ELW 344, LSB 442)

Theodulf of Orléans (ca. 760–821), born to a Gothic family in Spain, came to Charlemagne's realm as a Benedictine abbot and then the bishop of Orléans. He was an able administrator, a trusted theologian (see the *Libri Carolini*), and a prolific poet. Of his many verses, one has come down through the ages as central to Palm Sunday processions: "All Glory, Laud, and Honor." The hymn text is taken from the start of a larger poem (12 of the 78 lines), with clear reference to Psalm 24:7–10 and to the Palm Sunday gospel texts (Matthew 21:9, Luke 19:38, also echoing Psalm 118:26). The opening lines become the refrain: "All glory, laud, and honor to you, redeemer, king, to whom the lips of children made sweet hosanna ring." The five stanzas accurately reflect the next ten lines of the poem, but the rest of the text also deserves attention, for reasons historical and fanciful.

As abbot, bishop, and theological advisor, Theodulf served Charles well, but when the Great emperor died in 814, his sons fought and the empire splintered and suffered. Louis (the Pious) thought Theodulf disloyal to his claims and had the aging bishop deposed and incarcerated in 817. From a comment in the latter part of this poem, Theodulf apparently wrote it while imprisoned in a monastic cell in Angers, where his death in 821 leaves sad testimony to a troubled realm. Much later, a more cheerful fable arose, namely, that Louis the Pious on a Palm Sunday visit to Angers heard Theodulf singing this hymn from his cell and was moved to have the poet released and the hymn sung every Palm Sunday. Translator John Mason Neale liked that fictional happy ending and also smiled at the later line: "Be Thou, O Lord, the Rider, and we the little ass."[16]

---

16   *An Annotated Anthology of Hymns*, ed. J. R. Watson (Oxford: Oxford University Press, 2002), 37.

All Glory, Laud, and Honor

Refrain

All glo - ry, laud, and hon - or to you, re - deem - er, king,

to whom the lips of chil - dren made sweet ho - san - nas ring.

1 You are the king of Is - rael and Da - vid's roy - al Son,
2 The com - pa - ny of an - gels are prais - ing you on high;
3 The mul - ti - tude of pil - grims with palms be - fore you went;
4 To you, be - fore your pas - sion, they sang their hymns of praise.
5 Their prais - es you ac - cept - ed; ac - cept the prayers we bring,

Refrain

now in the Lord's name com - ing, our King and Bless - ed One.
cre - a - tion and all mor - tals in cho - rus make re - ply.
our praise and prayer and an - thems be - fore you we pre - sent.
To you, now high ex - alt - ed, our mel - o - dy we raise.
great au - thor of all good - ness, O good and gra - cious King.

Text: Theodulph of Orleans, c. 760–821; tr. John Mason Neale, 1818–1866, alt.
Music: VALET WILL ICH DIR GEBEN. Melchior Teschner, 1584–1635

"Creator Spirit" (ELW 577–78, LSB 498–99) and the *Filioque*
The other hymn from this Carolingian context is more complex, theologically and ecumenically. The doctrinal issue again involves the Nicene Creed, but this time in the third article, on the Holy Spirit. The most plausible author is the immensely learned and accomplished Benedictine abbot and bishop, Rhabanus Maurus (ca. 780–856), although this attribution falls short of proof or total consensus.[17] *Veni, Creator Spiritus* (Come, Creator Spirit) has been sung at Pentecost services, ordinations, and special church gatherings for centuries, whether in its elegant and compact Latin text, in German versions such as Martin Luther's 1524 translation (LW 53: 260) or in English as "Come, Holy Ghost, Our Souls Inspire" (tr. John Cosin, LBW 472–73), "Creator Spirit, Heavenly Dove" (ELW 577–78), or "Come, Holy Ghost, Creator Blest" (LSB 498–99). See also John Dryden's poetic paraphrase (LSB 500). It has also been sung in the monastic daily office, specifically at Terce or the "third hour" of the day when the Holy Spirit came upon the disciples (Acts 2:15). Even the plainsong chant tune, nicely matched to this text throughout its history, is a classic.

Sometimes considered the first Latin hymn about the Holy Spirit, the text starts with a surprise, builds on Scripture, and ends with a subtle glimpse of an ecumenical impasse still in place. We might not expect the Holy Spirit to be called "Creator," but Psalm 104:30 ("When you send forth your Spirit, they are created") puts it that way, and St. Ambrose had emphasized the point. The title of Comforter (st. 2) and mention of the sevenfold gift (st. 3) are also based on Scripture (John 14:16 and 16:7; Isaiah 11:2). The mention of God's hand in stanza 3 is more complex, for the Latin text actually specifies the Spirit as "the finger on God's right hand," combining Luke 11:20 and Matthew 12:28. Calling the Holy Spirit to come upon the faithful as life, fire, love, light, and peace deploys a multitude of uncontested biblical

---

17   See the discussion of authorship in *LSB Companion*, 498–99.

Creator Spirit, Heavenly Dove

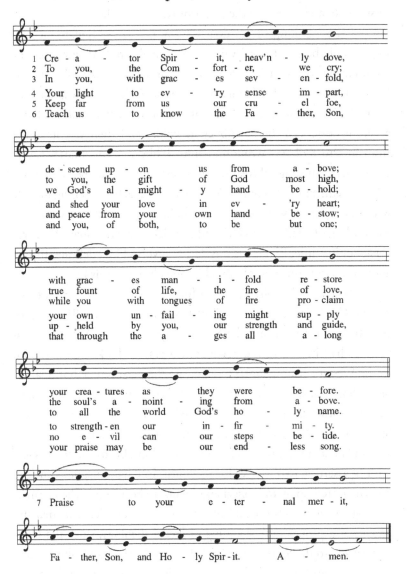

1 Cre - a - tor Spir - it, heav'n - ly dove,
2 To you, the Com - fort - er, we cry;
3 In you, with grac - es sev - en - fold,
4 Your light to ev - 'ry sense im - part,
5 Keep far from us our cru - el foe,
6 Teach us to know the Fa - ther, Son,

de - scend up - on us from a - bove;
to you, the gift of God most high,
we God's al - might - y hand be - hold;
and shed your love in ev - 'ry heart;
and peace from your own hand be - stow;
and you, of both, to be but one;

with grac - es man - i - fold re - store
true fount of life, the fire of love,
while you with tongues of fire pro - claim
your own un - fail - ing might sup - ply
up - held by you, our strength and guide,
that through the a - ges all a - long

your crea - tures as they were be - fore.
the soul's a - noint - ing from a - bove.
to all the world God's ho - ly name.
to strength - en our in - fir - mi - ty.
no e - vil can our steps be - tide.
your praise may be our end - less song.

7 Praise to your e - ter - nal mer - it,

Fa - ther, Son, and Ho - ly Spir - it. A - men.

Text: Rhabanus Maurus, 776–856; tr. composite
Music: VENI CREATOR SPIRITUS, Sarum plainsong, mode VIII

attributes, but a complex story of ecumenical disagreement is glimpsed in stanza 6, and intersects the career of Rhabanus Maurus.

If the Carolingian era deserves any talk of a "Renaissance," it might apply best to the revival of educational standards for monastic communities (by then, all Benedictine) and clergy, as well as to the imperial court itself. Rhabanus, born around 780, was educated by the learned Alcuin. He became head of the prominent monastic school at the historic Benedictine Abbey at Fulda, and then was its abbot from 822 to 842. He wrote numerous biblical commentaries (using the Fathers), theological treatises, and especially encyclopedic tools for religious education, becoming known as the Teacher of Germany. He wrote poetry too, some of it in symbolic shapes such as crosses. As Archbishop of Mainz from 847 and a leader in the theological controversies of his time, Rhabanus was deeply involved in a delicate dispute about the Holy Spirit, as glimpsed in one phrase of this hymn.

Did the Holy Spirit "proceed from the Father" as in the official Nicene Creed from the Council of Constantinople in 381, or "proceed from the Father and the Son" (*filioque*) as some Western Latin versions had it? Again, the Arian controversy is the key background. In the Western realm, efforts to eradicate the persistent subordination of the Son as less than the Father had led some to add the Son alongside the Father in this part of the creed, so that they would be equal in honor. But the Eastern Orthodox theologians objected not only to any unilateral addition to the official creed but also to the theological error of asserting two sources for the Spirit. In Charlemagne's time the dispute heated up, with biblical arguments on both sides. The German theologians at the 809 Synod of Aachen, for example, defended the *filioque* as a proper understanding of credal theology, since the Holy Spirit was also the Spirit of Christ, being sent by the Son (John 15.26). But the Byzantine theologians insisted that the sending of the Spirit within history was not the same as the Spirit's eternal procession from the Father. Some of them even started to insist that the Spirit proceeded "from the Father alone."

That the hymn text here refers to the Spirit "of both," meaning the Spirit of the Father and of the Son, might seem to be an endorsement of a Western insistence upon the *filioque* clause and an eternal double procession. But it could also be a careful avoidance of an issue that was contested not only between East and West but also within the Western realm itself. After all, the popes, including Leo III who crowned Charlemagne, agreed that the original wording, without the *filioque,* should prevail in the creed, at least in Rome. Thus papal practice was set against the German imperial line, even if they all agreed on the theological substance of the matter. The hymn text seems to avoid the exact credal language: "Teach us to know the Father, Son, and you, of both to be but one," literally, "Spirit of them both" (*te utriusque Spiritum*). Both the Latin and the Greek theologians could say, with Scripture, that the Spirit of God was the Spirit of the Father (Matthew 10:20, Ephesians 2:18) and of the Son (Acts 16.7, Romans 8:9, Galatians 4:6, Philippians 1:19), and thus "of both." But they did not agree about the eternal procession of the Spirit from both the Father and the Son. Western authorities agreed on the double procession as a theological matter, but the Pope's diplomatic position at the time was that the Nicene Creed itself should not carry this expansion. Thus, a careful German teacher and Roman bishop like Rhabanus might thread the poetic needle by crafting a non-committal phrase where the German Emperor's theologians and the Roman Pope's position had common ground, since he was not quoting a creed. In other words, perhaps he intentionally avoided being too explicit.

The dispute over the procession of the Holy Spirit is worth attention today because it is still unresolved. In the eleventh century, the popes did add the phrase to the Nicene Creed for use in Rome, and they quickly accused the Eastern Church of dropping the *filioque* even though it never had been part of the original text of the creed. Subsequent efforts at reconciliation, such as the 1274 Council of Lyon, failed to resolve the rupture, although the proposed compromise language of "*through* the Son" has been revived in some modern discussions. The *filioque* remains a stumbling block, and indeed the single largest doctrinal barrier between Eastern Orthodox churches of all kinds and the Western churches, whether Roman Catholic or Protestant.[18] As in the creed itself with *filioque*, a single word in a hymn like *utriusque* can reflect an enormous topic. Meanwhile, the hymn is still sung at ordinations, the beginnings of some church assemblies, and even in a few concert halls, as in Gustav Mahler's Eighth Symphony.

A *Do-Re-Mi* Excursus

Before leaving this early medieval cluster of less familiar names and anonymous hymns, a musical example deserves a note, so to speak. It has been used by music teachers across the centuries and around the world, and usually without mentioning anything medieval. Although our topic is church history by way of sung texts and not the music itself, the medieval origin of *do-re-mi* warrants an exception. A hymn for John the Baptist loosely attributed to the learned eighth-century Benedictine Paul the Deacon was adapted by a renowned music instructor around the turn of the millennium, namely, Guido d'Arezzo (ca. 990–1033). In his hands the opening phrases of *Ut queant laxis* started on successive notes of the scale: *ut, re* for *resonare, mi* for *mira, fa* for *famuli,* and so forth. Guido's successful teaching methods, including a diagram of the human hand as a memory aid, became standard in music instruction for centuries. With an early modern switch of *ut* to become *do,* the stage was set for music lessons into the present, as popularized by Sister Maria in *The Sound of Music.*

---

18   For a brief introduction to the *filioque* history and theology, see John Meyendorff, "Filioque," *The Dictionary of the Middle Ages* 5: 62–63.

5

SAINTS BERNARD, FRANCIS, AND THOMAS AQUINAS

The High Middle Ages (1100–1300)

"What language shall I borrow?"

WITH THE "HIGH" Middle Ages, we meet the more familiar names of Saints Bernard of Clairvaux, Francis of Assisi, and Thomas Aquinas, all with some well-known hymns. The twelfth century (1100–1200) presents a dilemma for any narrator and an irony regarding hymnody. The dilemma is that this century is so packed with momentous developments, including the Crusades and the rise of Gothic architecture—and such vivid and productive personalities, including Abbot Bernard and Abbess Hildegard of Bingen, plus the famous Abelard and Heloise—that one narrative can hardly cover it all. The irony is that for all its creativity in literature and the arts, there are hardly any hymns from this packed century in general use today. Further, the most prominent figure of the age, Bernard of Clairvaux, did not write hymns himself, though he was later credited with some famous ones, like "O Sacred Head, Now Wounded."

Two of the most recognized and significant phenomena of the Middle Ages as a whole, the Crusades and Gothic architecture, stem from not only the same time and place—the 1100s in France—but also from the same situation: a booming population and economy. Crusading and construction on this scale were both extraordinarily expensive, and happened only because there were fiscal resources and ambitions to match. Western Europe seemed to be bulging at the seams, both pushing out beyond its borders, taking back Sicily and parts of Spain from Islamic rule and forging on to Jerusalem, and also rising up into the sky in the ever-higher spires and cathedrals later called "Gothic." Literature and culture also expanded dramatically, including theology and music. Why all this happened at this particular time and place remains speculative. Perhaps a slight improvement in the weather and thus the growing season, with larger crops for the food supply, led to better health and a growth spurt in the population and the economy. In any case, it was a boom time in Western Europe and hard to summarize quickly.

Saint Bernard of Clairvaux and the Twelfth Century

Bernard of Clairvaux

For all the developments and celebrities of the age, one figure emerges as the hub connected to them all: Bernard of Clairvaux (1090–1153), abbot and author. You could call Saint Bernard the "big dog" of the twelfth century, although the Swiss name for those large canines comes from a different Bernard. His connection to the emergence of a new style of church building was not as its advocate but as an ascetic critic of its ostentatious decoration and luxury. He did not launch what became known as the First Crusade (1096–1100) but advocated and preached the Second (1147). He was a key correspondent-supporter of Hildegard, and a fierce critic-opponent of Abelard. Amid all this, his sermons and devotional writings became so cherished and popular that many adopted his themes and style, even putting his name on works not his.

Bernard was part of a reform movement in Western monasticism, providing another variation on the Benedictine theme. The original sixth-century mantra had been "worship and work." The Cluny reform of Benedictine life from the tenth century on pursued a heavy emphasis on worship, to the neglect of manual labor. At least, so thought some reformers around 1100 called Cistercians, an energetic youth movement epitomized by Bernard. Their campaign for honest work and simpler worship, yet still within the daily office of Psalms and hymns, meant success in attracting members and at industrious farming. Their communities thrived. When Abbot Suger of St. Denis, a traditional Benedictine, rebuilt his abbey church in an impressive new style that was soon called "Gothic" by critics who preferred the Roman (Romanesque) tradition, Cistercians like Bernard looked askance at the lavish luxury involved. The new buildings, such as Notre Dame in Paris and Chartres Cathedral later in the twelfth century, were impressive—and still are, as evident in the global dismay at the former's devastating fire in 2019. Such buildings inspired elaborate liturgies, including musical innovations such as polyphony, but not much hymnody sung today.

Bernard's energy and charisma led him as the Abbot of the Cistercian house at Clairvaux to become a powerful figure in French life, and not just in the church. Even King Louis VII and Queen Eleanor of Aquitaine asked his advice, and together went on the Second Crusade that Bernard had advocated. Aquitaine was the land of troubadour ballads, and the Crusades inspired songs of chivalry too, but such music did not translate into hymns. Upon their return from the Holy Land, Louis and Eleanor divorced, and she quickly married Henry II King of England, a tale that continued with their son Richard the Lion-hearted and then the stories and songs of Robin Hood.

Hildegard of Bingen

Bernard's fame as a counselor also led to extensive correspondence far beyond France. When Hildegard of Bingen (1098–1179) wondered whether to put her visions and voices into a book, she wrote to the esteemed Abbot of Clairvaux for advice. He encouraged her to write them down, and when her first book (*Scivias*) came to the attention of Pope Eugenius III, he too approved. Normally a pope would be more influential than an abbot, but the abbot in this case was still the spiritual advisor to this Cistercian pope, who had been his monk at Clairvaux. Here and in general, Bernard was more influential than even the popes of his time. Hildegard's *Scivias* ended with some of the songs she had composed, both text and music, and there were dozens more later in her long and amazing career. One composition, the *Ordo Virtutum,* was like an opera, a play that was sung entirely by women; the male devil, lacking God's gift of music, has only a speaking part. Although Hildegard's songs were too elaborate and difficult to become hymns, some have been revived for recordings and concert halls today. However, some of her various phrases about the Holy Spirit have been combined by Jean Janzen in "O Holy Spirit, Root of Life" (ELW 399).

Bernard's theological writings were mostly expositions of Scripture, both sermons and spiritual guidance in general. In that sense he was a traditionalist, and he opposed some of the new methods proposed by Peter Abelard (1079–1143). The love story of Abelard and Heloise (ca. 1100–63) often overshadows the intellectual creativity shown by both in their writings, including Abelard's many poems and songs. In fact, Abelard was one of the great hymn writers of the twelfth century, creating over one hundred hymns for the daily office and the church year, and many were written specifically for the monastic community where Heloise was the learned abbess. Only one of Abelard's hymns has enjoyed continued use into the present: *O quanta qualia*, "Oh, What Their Joy" (LBW 337, LSB 675).[1] Bernard's part in this saga pertains to the heresy charges he pursued against Abelard's more philosophical and speculative theology, not the love affair or the hymn texts.

There is one more twelfth-century development to note, also with considerable hymn production and yet little legacy for it. Wedged between the contrasting caricatures of Bernard the devout monk and Abelard the intellectual professor, one community wanted to combine the two roles. The Abbey of St. Victor in Paris was both a community of prayerful discipline and also a school of productive and creative theologians. After Bernard's respected contemporaries William of Champeaux and Hugh of St. Victor had established this combination, others carried it forward, such as Adam of St. Victor in the later twelfth century. He too composed many sung texts, especially Sequences attached to the Alleluia, but here again they have not endured as hymns. One of them, "Hail, O Mother of our Savior," indicates the rise of attention and hymnody addressed to the Virgin Mary in this century, a topic that was also one of Bernard's themes.[2]

---

1   See also "Alone thou goest forth," Routley-Richardson, *Panorama* #549, p. 441, and many more of Abelard's texts in Walsh, *Hymns,* #78–90.

2   Walsh, *Hymns,* #91.

Coming back to Bernard, we find him surrounded by songs old and new, monastics and troubadours, but not himself the author of hymns. His poetic sermonic style, however, inspired many others, with two specific poems looming large in the history of hymnody. One long poem, *Dulcis Jesu Memoria*, lives on in multiple short hymns: "Jesus, the Very Thought of You" (ELW 754 and LBW 316), "O Jesus, Joy of Loving Hearts" (ELW 658 and LBW 356), and "O Jesus, King Most Wonderful" (LSB 554 and LBW 537). An even longer poem has a yet larger afterlife in "O Sacred Head, Now Wounded" (ELW 351 and LSB 449–50) as well as "Wide Open are your Hands" (LBW 489). However, the connection to Bernard is loose and needs thematic context.

What inspired Bernard's hearers, contemporaries, and posterity was his eloquent emphasis on love. He wrote about different kinds of love, but especially human love for Christ the heavenly bridegroom, crucified for us. His sermons on the Song of Songs were famous examples, along with a treatise *On Loving God*. Our interest is in the overlap of Bernard's scriptural rhapsody on such love with some hymn texts attributed to him. Yet even a surprising argument like "Crusading as an Act of Love," meaning love for the persecuted Christians in the Holy Land, invokes Bernard's support for the Crusades in terms of love.[3] The key context here, for both Bernard's corpus and also the hymns under his name, is the Christian tradition of interpreting the Song of Songs as a love affair between the Christian soul and Christ the heavenly bridegroom, including his handsome body displayed on the cross.

Dulcis Jesu Memoria Hymns (ELW 754 and ELW 658, LSB 554)

A single long poem associated with the twelfth-century Cistercian movement stands behind several brief hymns in modern usage that are sometimes attributed to Bernard. *Dulcis Jesu Memoria* expresses its theme in the very title: "the sweet memory of Jesus." "Jesus, the Very

---

3   The phrase is from the title of Jonathan Riley-Smith's essay, "Crusading as an Act of Love," *History* 65 (1980): 177–192. See any of his several books on the Crusades.

Thought of You" (ELW 754) presents the opening stanzas of a translation of the whole poem by Edward Caswall. Like John Mason Neale, Caswall was part of the Oxford Movement's retrieval of Latin hymns in the nineteenth century. "O Jesus, Joy of Loving Hearts" (ELW 658) is a translation of some of the same poem's other stanzas by Ray Palmer (1808–87), American author of "My Faith Looks Up to Thee." Caswall's translation of this poem is also used in the other stanzas chosen for "O Jesus, King Most Wonderful" (LBW 537, LSB 554).

As seen even in the titles of these hymns, the poem's theme of love for Jesus is expressed in highly personal and emotional terms: sweet delight, the joy of loving hearts. Although the attribution to Bernard is contested, the theme matches his well-known emphasis on love, especially the soul's love for Jesus. His dozens of sermons on the Song of Songs made it personal: the tender and ardent love of the bride/soul for the handsome bridegroom/Christ. (On some occasions, the referents were the loving mother Mary and the beloved son Jesus.) Bernard did not invent this interpretation of the scriptural book that is today associated mostly with weddings. It stems from Origen of Alexandria's third-century observation that the biblical bride may be a corporate reference to Israel or the church, as throughout Scripture, or an individual reference to the soul. Bernard's eloquent expansion on this theme is also summed up in his treatise *On Loving God.* God's prior love stimulates the soul's love for Christ, in terms of affection, desire, and sweetness, as in the hymns. Even if Bernard's authorship of *Dulcis Jesu Memoria* is not certain, there are striking overlaps of phrases with this known work. In Bernard's treatise: "O Lord, you are so good to the soul who seeks you, What must you be to the one who finds you?" From Caswell's translation of "Jesus, the Very Thought of Thee": "How good [thou art] to those who seek! But what to those who find?"[4]

---

4   *On Loving God* VII, 22; *Readings,* Coakley and Sterk, 349. The hymn is unfortunately abridged at this point in ELW 754 and LBW 316, but the passage is available elsewhere, as in *Service Book and Hymnal* (Minneapolis: Augsburg Publishing House,

"O Sacred Head, Now Wounded" (ELW 351–52, LSB 449–50)

The other long poem behind yet further hymns attributed to Bernard has less claim on his authorship but more prominence in congregational and classical music. *Salve, mundi salutare* hails various parts of the Savior's crucified body, such as the hands and especially the head. German and then English translations have made it famous as "O Sacred Head, Now Wounded," including multiple compositions by J. S. Bach. The influence of Bernard's personal, loving devotion to Christ the heavenly bridegroom prevails in the Cistercian and then the Franciscan literature of the next century and far beyond. *Salve, mundi salutare* voices this devotion in successive sections addressed to Christ's feet, knees, hands, side, and face or head. Although long attributed to Bernard, its oldest manuscript (1320) names Arnulf of Louvain (ca. 1200–ca. 1250), a Cistercian abbot in Brabant/Belgium. Two further sections, to Christ's breast and heart, were apparently added later to make seven hymns for the seven days of Holy Week.

The poem evokes the visual field of a crucifix, directing contemplation to several suffering features of Christ's body on the cross. The knees, for example, bloodied on the way to the cross, may seem an unlikely focus of spiritual comfort, but the poet reminds the hearer/viewer of another biblical scene: you will be pulled unto his lap and cherished on those knees as beloved children. The section on the wounded hands was paraphrased very loosely by the nineteenth-century American Lutheran Charles Porterfield Krauth as "Wide Open Are Your Hands" (LBW 489). Krauth strayed from the poet's words but stayed faithful to Bernard's theme. "Wide open are your hands To pay with more than gold The awful debt of guilt and sin, Forever and of old. Ah, let me grasp those hands, That we may never part, And let the power of their blood Sustain my fainting heart. Wide open are your arms, A fallen world to embrace . . ."

1958), 481 at stanzas 3–4; to be cited as SBH. See also *Glory to God* 629, and Routley-Richardson, *Panorama* #163B, p. 155.

Moving up to the side wound and then the face or head, through such evocative verbal and visual images the soul can be "caught up" in rapturous contemplation. Bernard himself spoke of the bliss of losing oneself in an apparent union with God, later called mystical ecstasy. Just as novels or movies today can pull us into a story and thus out of ourselves, which is the literal meaning of "ecstasy," so a medieval poem and crucifix could pull believers into the passion story in powerful ways.

This captivating story reaches its full effect and greatest legacy in the section about the face or head. Despite dropped stanzas and sanitizing translations, the hymn has retained a firm hold on congregational usage, especially with the melody that was attached to the German version and has lived on in variations from J. S. Bach to Paul Simon. Originally in five ten-line sections yielding ten stanzas, the text as used in modern hymnals has been steadily reduced. *The Lutheran Hymnal* in 1941 had all ten stanzas; the *Lutheran Service Book* today has one version in four stanzas and another in seven (LSB 449 and 450). A Norwegian-American Lutheran hymnal had eight stanzas in 1913 (*Lutheran Hymnary*, Augsburg Publishing House #315); then that same publisher's *Service Book and Hymnal* in 1958 had only four (as followed by the LBW and ELW), and the *Presbyterian Hymnal* had only three in 1990 (followed by the *Glory to God* in 2013).

But the story of translating this hymn is more complex than a tale of disappearing stanzas. The centerpiece of the story is the German translation and paraphrase of this entire section of the poem by Paul Gerhardt (1607–76). It was quickly and firmly attached to a German melody, aptly from a love song, that had been adapted earlier by Hans Hassler (1564–1612) for different texts. Gerhardt's major career as Lutheran pastor and poet/hymn writer includes many other beloved hymns from seventeenth-century Germany that will be covered later. His pastorate in Mittenwalde south of Berlin meant seeing the face of Christ every week in a rendition of Veronica's veil.[5] This text, his most

5   *LSB Companion*, vol. 2, 346.

famous, became not only a standard in German hymnals since 1656 but also regularly appeared in J. S. Bach's works: heavily in the St. Matthew Passion and also in oratorios and cantatas. English translations stem more from the German hymn than from the Latin poem, as seen in the widely used version by James Waddell Alexander (1804–59), an American Presbyterian who also translated all ten stanzas. The evolution from Latin to German to English has attracted scholarly attention, for example, in the cleaning up of the spit and blood.[6] The Latin poem as received started brutally. "Hail, bloodied head, all crowned with thorns, shattered, wounded, so beaten by the rod, face smeared with spit." Gerhardt's translation tones this beating down a notch, but it retains the blood and wounds, even in the title "O Haupt voll Blut und Wunden" (O head covered with blood and wounds). Alexander's version drops the blood entirely, but the head is still wounded and gory. "O sacred head, now wounded, with grief and shame weighed down, now scornfully surrounded with thorns, thine only crown; O sacred head, what glory, what bliss till now was thine! Yet, though despised and gory, I joy to call thee mine."

Gerhardt's poetic license adapted the original, and inspired Alexander's creativity as well, but the theological core stems from the original Latin poem and indeed from Bernard's own emphases. For example, what has become the second stanza's conclusion (ELW 351, st. 2, from st. 4 of Gerhardt and Alexander) expresses loving gratitude for the saving atonement of the cross. Christ's suffering was for sinners' gain; "Mine, mine was the transgression, but thine the deadly pain." This tracks Gerhardt's wording, "I myself bear the blame for all that you have borne," itself a translation faithful to the Latin original, "Killed this way because of me, a sinner of indignity."

Alexander's version has its own eloquence, beyond the sources but faithful to their spirit of Bernardine warmth. "What language shall I

---

6   George Faithful, "A More Brotherly Song, a Less Passionate Passion," *Church History* 82.4 (2013): 779–811. For Latin, German, and English versions, albeit not all stanzas, see Routley-Richardson, *Panorama* #194, pp. 193–196.

O Sacred Head, Now Wounded

1 O sa - cred head, now wound - ed, with grief and shame weighed down,
2 How pale thou art with an - guish, with sore a - buse and scorn;
3 What lan - guage shall I bor - row to thank thee, dear - est friend,
4 Lord, be my con - so - la - tion; shield me when I must die;

now scorn - ful - ly sur - round - ed with thorns, thine on - ly crown;
how does thy face now lan - guish, which once was bright as morn!
for this thy dy - ing sor - row, thy pit - y with - out end?
re - mind me of thy pas - sion when my last hour draws nigh.

O sa - cred head, what glo - ry, what bliss till now was thine!
Thy grief and bit - ter pas - sion were all for sin - ners' gain;
Oh, make me thine for - ev - er, and should I faint - ing be,
These eyes, new faith re - ceiv - ing, from thee shall nev - er move;

Yet, though de - spised and gor - y, I joy to call thee mine.
mine, mine was the trans-gres - sion, but thine the dead - ly pain.
Lord, let me nev - er, nev - er out - live my love to thee.
for all who die be - liev - ing die safe - ly in thy love.

Text: Paul Gerhardt, 1607–1676, based on Arnulf of Louvain, d. 1250; tr. composite
Music: HERZLICH TUT MICH VERLANGEN, German melody, c. 1500; adapt. Hans Leo Hassler, 1564–1612;
    arr. Johann Sebastian Bach, 1685–1750

borrow, to thank thee, dearest friend, for this thy dying sorrow, thy pity without end?" (sometimes st. 3, originally st. 8). At the end, the Presbyterian's version has been edited further but retains a key medieval theme from the original Cistercian context as also preserved by the Lutheran Gerhardt. Looking upon the crucified Christ can be consolation in the face of one's own death, as exemplified not only by the plague-ridden age of Gerhardt but also earlier by Julian of Norwich (1342–1430?). Mortally ill in the wake of the Black Death of the fourteenth century, she was counseled to look at a crucifix. Upon surviving, she shared the extraordinary experience in her *Showings,* and in a way that confirms the hymn's finale, if we make a gender change. "These eyes, new faith receiving, From thee shall never move; for *she* who dies believing, dies safely in thy love." Julian's own comments about Jesus as mother are loosely adapted to the triune God in "Mothering God" (ELW 735), by Jean Janzen.

Based upon Bernard's own devotion to Christ, the Latin poem turned German and American hymn is also of broader ecumenical interest. In Alexander's time, American Protestants were severely anti-Catholic and not at all disposed to welcome anything monastic or from the Middle Ages. Yet, following Luther and John Calvin's own high regard for Bernard as a church father, a poem about Christ attributed to the medieval abbot was welcomed and sung even by anti–Roman Catholics. Further, Hassler's tune has brought the hymn not only to diverse church services and concert halls worldwide by way of Bach's genius but also to popular music in new texts and arrangements as sung by Peter, Paul and Mary in the 1960s as well as Paul Simon's "American Tune" in 1973. Saint Bernard's legacy has been broad and long, in writings genuine and otherwise.

From the Twelfth to the Thirteenth Century

Bernard's leadership of the Cistercians contributed to the material success of medieval monasticism and Latin Christendom in general. As represented by Gothic super-structures such as Chartres Cathedral and by the Crusades such as the "Third" in 1187–90 that failed to retake Jerusalem, the age was awash in extra money. Like Western Europe overall, the Benedictine-Cistercian abbeys and the church also grew wealthy, so much so that for some it became a spiritual virtue to choose extreme poverty. A French merchant named Valdes (Waldo) and the "Poor of Lyons" in France championed such poverty and extreme simplicity around 1180. At first approved by the church, Waldo and his followers then ran afoul of the bishop's prohibition of unauthorized preaching. The Waldensians, as they became known, were thus branded heretics. Yet, they survived the persecutions and will tell you today that St. Francis was not so original.

Francis of Assisi (1182–1226)

Francis of Assisi

A song about "Brother Sun, Sister Moon" may sound too Green to be medieval, or perhaps more "hippie" than historical, as in the 1973 film by that name. But the famous Francis of Assisi did indeed compose that canticle, and his deep appreciation for nature stemmed from living mostly outdoors after renouncing his family wealth.

As with Valdes/Waldo, for Francis, and then for Clare of Assisi, the virtue amid the wealth of their context was not in being poor but rather in *becoming* poor, voluntarily, in imitation of Christ and not within a securely funded community. Not for Francis was the stability of a Benedictine house with a roof over his head and food on the table. Francis and Clare renounced the wealth of their culture, their town, and their families, and thereby inspired numerous followers, both immediately and also through the centuries into the present. Unlike Waldo, Francis secured the support of his bishop and approval from the pope, as did Clare. With Francis, it is hard to separate the actual life from the legendary image. Historical facts are mixed with fanciful fiction, and the legends have become part of the legacy. But the core of his story is firm: he renounced wealth and chose a beggar's life of simplicity and poverty. It is also firm that the poem we sing as "The Canticle of Brother Sun" really is by Francis, unlike later sayings and legends with their exaggerations.

Raised in a wealthy merchant's family, young Francis enjoyed life and even some military exploits until the hardship of illness as a prisoner of war shook him up. He renounced his property, defied his father, and took to the streets as a beggar in imitation of Christ. The resulting simplicity of a life spent mostly outdoors had many results, including the rapport with creation expressed in this canticle. Leaving the military behind to become a prophet of peace, however, is complicated by his participation in the Fifth Crusade in 1219. That he only wanted to have peace talks with the Sultan, a meeting that spawned medieval legends of its own, supports the mention of peace in the hymn. But the prayer "Make me an instrument of your peace" is a modern invention, first in French and from the early twentieth century, around 1912. In and around Assisi, with a few followers and in regular contact with the lepers as fellow beggars, Francis lived under the sun and close to the ground. Tales of preaching to the birds and pacifying "The Very Fierce Wolf of Gubbio" grew up later, but he was clearly close to creation and the natural world, as evident in his canticle.

"All Creatures," The Canticle of Brother Sun (ELW 835)

The song by Francis has had many names but was called "The Canticle of Brother Sun" early on. The language is not Latin but the vernacular, an Umbrian dialect of Italian, as befits a ministry in Assisi's streets and countryside. In fact, this text is linguistically important as the earliest known Italian poem. The canticle stems from late in Francis's life, and some stanzas may have been added at the very end, with the mention of peaceful forgiveness and "our sister bodily death." The theme is clearly praise for the "most high" God, whom no person can name. But the Lord can be praised through God's creatures. The original phrase, repeated eight times, is *Laudato si', mi Signore,* "Be praised, my Lord," as addressed to God, not to the creatures themselves. But the praise is *through* (per) those creatures, and it moves down from the bright heavenly bodies to the traditional four elements and then to the human condition of infirmity and bodily death. Thus, after the strong address to God and the opening mention of "brother sun," the pattern recurs for many members of creation's family. For example, "Be praised, my Lord, through sister moon and the stars." Then the Lord is praised through the four created elements: brother wind, sister water, brother fire, and "our sister mother earth," each with specific attributes.

Francis thus sings the harmonious goodness of creation, not a discordant evil of matter. Although the praise is not *for* these creatures, nor are they themselves being asked to praise God, an initial line ("Be praised, my Lord, *with* all your creatures") contains both possibilities. Some translations, like William Draper's "All Creatures of Our God and King" (LBW 527), reflect the biblical model of Psalm 148 as well as the apocryphal "Song/Ode of the Three Jews" (Greek Daniel 3:51–90) in addressing an invitation *to* these creatures, so that all creation joins in praise of God.

Apparently reflecting a resolved quarrel in Assisi, one late stanza adds mention of those who forgive in peace. Even bodily death is added as "our sister" in this mortal realm, as Francis after long and painful illnesses faced his own end. The continuation of that thought is rarely in any hymnal: "Woe to those who die in mortal sin. Blessed are those whom death will find in Your most holy will, for the second death shall do them no harm."[7] Here, as in the forgiveness portion, some translators add explicit mention of Christ (LBW 527, st. 6; ELW 835, stanzas 4–5), although Francis had none. At the end, the canticle switches to a plural address, calling all to praise and bless the Lord in the "Benedicite" terms of Psalm 148 and the Song of the Three Jews. The last word is a very Franciscan "humility," but modern hymnals often add a fully trinitarian doxology.

Draper's translation, with all the alleluias echoing the Psalms, was nicely matched with a much older tune in 1919, and thus became influential, even if it later needed editing to restore all the familial language for creation (for example, ELW 835). Francis's original wording has also seen a general revival because of contemporary concern for mother earth. Even taking the saint's name, Pope Francis issued his early encyclical in 2015 under the title " 'Laudato Si': On Care for our Common Home." Whether loosely paraphrased or cited by the original wording, the Canticle of Brother Sun has had a powerful presence in modern hymnals and the current concern for creation.

With such a message and as an inspiring Christlike model, indeed one whose contemplation on Christ crucified was so intense that he himself famously received the same wounds, Francis naturally attracted followers. A few young men begging around Assisi posed no problem, especially since Francis had been embraced by the bishop. As his cohort grew, Francis asked and received support from Pope Innocent III in 1209. Although the Benedictine order was the norm, a Franciscan exception was granted: the "Order of the Lesser Brothers." By the time of his death in 1226, Francis had so many followers that administrative organization was needed, but that posed two particular challenges.

---

7   From *Francis and Clare, the Complete Works,* trans. R. Armstrong and I. Brady (New York: Paulist Press, 1982), 38–39. For the Italian text and English translations, see Routley-Richardson, *Panorama* #204, pp. 211–13. For a fuller discussion of Francis, including his focus on Christ crucified and his own stigmata, see Bernard McGinn, *The Presence of God,* vol. 3, *The Flowering of Mysticism* (New York: Crossroad, 1998), 54–55.

Clare of Assisi

First, a young woman in Assisi was inspired by Francis to renounce her familial wealth and to live in poverty. However, a woman begging on the streets was out of the question. The career of Clare of Assisi (ca. 1194–1253) is an essential key to Franciscan history. Francis supported Clare's vocation by giving her and her companions the dilapidated building he had been working on, and there she began the community where she lived the rest of her life. The second challenge stemmed from the sheer size of the following Francis attracted in many areas, and here too Clare played a part. A few men could beg and live on a town's streets, but hundreds and then thousands!? It was a challenge to observe the spiritual principle of strict poverty and yet to house large communities. The long history of internal Franciscan tensions between the Spirituals, later called Observants, and the Conventuals, as the labels had it, is beyond our scope, but Clare had a major role early on in fighting for absolute poverty in defense of the original vision. Even on her death bed she refused to accept the pope's compromises for the wording of her *Rule,* the charter for the network of communities later known as "The Poor Clares." The pope relented, her austere *Rule* was approved, and Clare promptly died, becoming quickly known in 1255 as Saint Clare of Assisi.

Besides the rich history of Francis and Clare and their followers, there is another outcome to note regarding poverty in this age of wealth. Alongside Francis, another inspirational figure championed poverty but with a different emphasis. Dominic (ca. 1172–1221) from Spain also advocated choosing to become poor, not only as a lifestyle in imitation of Christ but also and especially in commitment to a preaching ministry among the common people, according to the example of the original apostles. Thus, said he, heresies could be countered and the Christian message could be heard and accepted more readily. The Order of Preachers was the result, along with the Dominican women such as Catherine of Siena. To be good preachers, the Dominicans needed to be educated, and that leads us to the new schools of Scholasticism and to Thomas Aquinas and his hymnody.

Thomas Aquinas (1225–74)

Thomas Aquinas

The Dominican emphasis on education matched the era's expansion of theological schools, both schools of thought and places of learning. The older model of a cathedral school, for a specific region and under a bishop's authority, made room for a new type of school, more independent and attracting scholars from many quarters. Abelard, in the booming twelfth century, represents the early stages of this development in Paris. By the early thirteenth century, the time of Francis and Dominic, the University of Paris was a major center of theological learning.

When a young and talented Thomas chose the Dominican path, it was natural for him to leave his native area of Aquino near Naples to study with the order's famous teacher in Paris. Albert was called "the Great" for his leadership not only in theology/philosophy but also in the natural sciences. Thomas became Albert's assistant and prize pupil, going on to pen masterworks of his own like the *Summa theologiae*, the sum of theology. Albert had championed the new school's use of new tools, namely, some works by Aristotle, and Thomas applied the Philosopher to liturgical theology, including in his sacramental poetry. Later centuries, especially the nineteenth and twentieth, made Thomas Aquinas famous for his systematic theology, that all things come from God and return to God through Christ. But he was also known in his own time for his spiritual and sacramental devotion, including the poetic texts that Pope Urban IV in 1264 asked him to write for the promotion of the feast of Corpus Christi (the Body of Christ). This complex poetry lives on in church life, especially in the dense and difficult *Pange, lingua* (Sing, my tongue). Probably also by Thomas is the brief *Adoro te devote* (Thee, we adore), although separate from the Corpus Christi texts. Together, these hymns illustrate how Thomas used Aristotle to understand the sacramental presence of Christ in the Mass under the terminology of "transubstantiation."

Of the several prayers and poems that Thomas wrote for the sacramental feast day of Corpus Christi, *Pange, lingua* is the best known, as also sung during the closing processional at the Holy Thursday Mass. It starts with an echo of Fortunatus from the sixth century: "Sing, my tongue, the mystery of the glorious body and the precious blood."[8] Thomas's complex sacramental theology is expressed

---

8   Walsh, *Hymns*, #98, Latin text at p. 362, my translation.

in compressed Latin poetry, "probably the densest and most difficult hymn ever written," declared Erik Routley.[9] Stanza 4 in John Mason Neale's translation can introduce the concept of transubstantiation. "Word made flesh, by word ordaining Very bread his flesh to be; We, in wine Christ's blood obtaining, And, if senses fail to see, Faith alone will wake those straining To behold the mystery" (LBW 120 st. 4, LSB 630 st. 4). The idea that our physical senses fail to discern the body and blood invokes Aristotle's distinction between something's sensory appearances and its underlying substance. In the Mass, the substance of the bread is believed to be changed into the substance of Christ's body even though the external appearances remain those of bread. Thus, the *trans*formation of the substance yields the terminology of transubstantiation, something Thomas treated at length in his *Summa theologiae* 3a, 73–83. The shorter hymn presents the same theology but more accessibly.

"Thee We Adore" (*Adoro te devote*; ELW 476, LSB 640)

Although not as definitively attributable to Thomas as the Corpus Christi hymns, *Adoro te devote* (Thee We Adore) has on its side good probability as to authorship and especially pedagogical and musical appeal as to continued usage. Originally in seven short stanzas, it offers biblical details, such as the penitent thief and the namesake "doubting" Thomas, and vivid imagery such as the red-breasted pelican thought to feed her brood with her own blood (LSB 640, st. 3), although these features are lost in many truncated translations. But even in the four-stanza version (ELW 476, LBW 199, *Glory to God* 495), Thomas's eucharistic devotion comes through clearly, especially in the original first person singular "I" version.

Hymnal renditions often skip from the opening to the last three stanzas (originally stanzas 5–7), but the dropped second stanza can help us with the concept of transubstantiation. The physical senses of sight,

---

9   Routley-Richardson, *Panorama*, p. 157.

Thee We Adore, O Savior

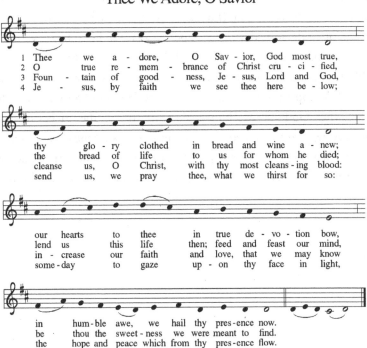

1 Thee we a - dore, O Sav - ior, God most true,
2 O true re - mem - brance of Christ cru - ci - fied,
3 Foun - tain of good - ness, Je - sus, Lord and God,
4 Je - sus, by faith we see thee here be - low;

thy glo - ry clothed in bread and wine a - new;
the bread of life to us for whom he died;
cleanse us, O Christ, with thy most cleans - ing blood:
send us, we pray thee, what we thirst for so:

our hearts to thee in true de - vo - tion bow,
lend us this life then; feed and feast our mind,
in - crease our faith and love, that we may know
some - day to gaze up - on thy face in light,

in hum - ble awe, we hail thy pres - ence now.
be thou the sweet - ness we were meant to find.
the hope and peace which from thy pres - ence flow.
blest ev - er - more with thy full glo - ry's sight. A - men.

Text: Thomas Aquinas, 1227–1274; tr. Gerard Manley Hopkins, 1844–1889, and James R. Woodford, 1820–1885, alt.
Music: ADORE TE DEVOTE, plainsong mode V; Processionale, Paris, 1697

touch, and taste may be deceived and thus fail to apprehend the changed substance beneath the attributes of bread, but faith comes from hearing Christ's word "This is my body." The genius of Thomas's poetry here calls for a genius poet-translator like Gerard Manley Hopkins.

> *Seeing, touching, tasting are in thee deceived;*
> *how says trusty hearing? That shall be believed;*
> *what God's Son hath told me, take for truth I do;*
> *truth himself speaks truly, or there's nothing true.*[10]

10   Gerard Manley Hopkins, *Collected Poems*, 1918, as cited in Routley-Richardson, *Panorama* #165C, p. 159.

The hymn ends with a prayer that parallels how the Dominicans understood the ending of Thomas's own life, namely, with the blessed vision of God: "someday to gaze upon thy face in light, blest evermore with thy full glory's sight." Shortly before dying just shy of fifty years old, Thomas had a health crisis and an experience of God's glory that meant he stopped writing his *Summa*. According to Dominican tradition, when God offered Thomas his heart's desire, the teacher replied, *non nisi te*, "nothing except you." Including this legendary example of fervent devotion, Thomas Aquinas with his doctrinal corpus and his sacramental poetry has had a long and deep influence on the Western church.

6

REFORMS BEFORE THE REFORMATION

The Late Middle Ages (1300–1500)

A "treasury" of medieval hymns

THE LATE MIDDLE Ages start off with the rich legacy of the Dominicans and Franciscans, including their many hymn texts, and end up illustrating many church reforms before what we usually call the Reformation. The era bequeathed a treasury of famous hymns, including "Oh, Love, How Deep, How Broad, How High," some of them explicitly adopted by Martin Luther.[1]

The followers of Francis and Dominic enriched and diversified the Western monastic literature considerably, including spiritual poetry by men and women. Alongside the Dominican Aquinas at the University of Paris was the Franciscan Bonaventure (ca. 1217–74), both a scholastic professor and a contemplative poet, as well as the head of his Order and the author of the official *Life of Francis.* Among the later "Poor Clares" was Angela of Foligno (ca. 1248–1309) whose ecstatic visions started in Assisi. The Dominican sisters also featured St. Catherine of Siena (1347–80), prolific Doctor (teacher) of the Church. Further, and bridging into the late medieval timeframe (1300–1500), two of the most famous medieval songs are also associated with Franciscans, namely, *Dies Irae* and *Stabat Mater.*

---

1   John Mason Neale, the major translator cited often already, expands on the language of treasury in an 1850 essay "English Hymnody," as quoted in *Hymns and Hymnody,* vol. 1, 170–171.

Dies Irae and Stabat Mater

Among the first companions of Francis and the author of early accounts of his extraordinary spiritual experiences was Thomas of Celano (ca. 1190–1260). He is also generally credited with writing the oft-sung Requiem Mass song *Dies Irae*, although he may have been expanding upon a prior text. Often translated and always praised for its compressed and evocative Latin, the song starts by quoting Zephaniah 1:15 about the last day: "That day will be a day of wrath." Indeed, echoing Matthew 24–25 and Revelation 20, wrath and trembling and fear dominate the early stanzas, but not the whole text. Starting with stanza 8, the "king of fearful majesty" is also called the "source of fondest love," and Christ is asked to share again the mercy he showed to Mary Magdalene and the penitent thief on the cross (st. 13). Added later to the original personal poem, apparently, was an ending more suitable for a corporate burial prayer, a plea for pity and rest. "Tearful will be that last day, when from ashes men will rise indicted and to be judged. Therefore, pity him, O God; O devoted Jesus, Lord, grant them eternal rest."[2] A severe abbreviation by Walter Scott has sometimes appeared in Protestant hymnals (SBH 298), but in general this hymn became part of the Roman Catholic Requiem Mass. Since Vatican II, the *Dies Irae* is rarely sung at such funerals, yet it lives on in concert oratorio form by a dozen great composers such as Mozart, Verdi, Berlioz, and Dvořák.

Another celebrated hymn stemming from the Bernardine and Franciscan devotion to Christ crucified and his grieving mother is *Stabat Mater*. It starts with the Latin text of John 19:25 ("his mother stood by the cross of Jesus") and expands on that scene's poignant sadness. Again, it was Edward Caswall whose translation has led the field. "At the cross her station keeping, stood the mournful Mother weeping, Close to Jesus to the last." The first four stanzas evoke the sorrow and suffering of mother and son, with the last six an

---

2   Walsh, *Hymns,* #95, p. 351.

intercessory prayer addressed to Mary herself: "Virgin of all virgins blest! Listen to my fond request: Let me share thy grief divine" (st. 8).[3] Protestant versions retain the opening quartet of descriptive stanzas, with some adjustments, but drop the multi-verse intercession addressed to Mary in favor of a final portion sung instead to Christ. For example, in some Lutheran hymnals the fifth stanza starts "Jesus, may her deep devotion Stir in me the same emotion" (SBH 84, LBW 110).

Still sung in full in Roman Catholic contexts such as the Lenten "Stations of the Cross," *Stabat Mater* was so popular in the Late Middle Ages that it attracted authorial claims for luminaries such as Bernard of Clairvaux, Bonaventure, and Pope Innocent III. Some important manuscripts name Jacopone da Todi (ca. 1236–1306), a Franciscan friar whose conversion late in life led to an outpouring of love poems about Christ on the cross. Most of his fervent verses are in Italian, not Latin, but his favorite themes fit this poem. In the end, *Stabat Mater* may be anonymous, as are so many late medieval hymns, but the text expresses the familiar Bernardine-Franciscan devotion to Christ. Here, too, famous composers such as Vivaldi, Haydn, Rossini, and Schubert have provided professional singers with multiple versions.

Late Medieval Hymns, Especially
for Advent through Pentecost

The Late Middle Ages have left us a large array of hymns sung today, some of them with attributions to named authors. But many more are anonymous. In fact, a congregation could sing anonymous late medieval hymns from Advent through Pentecost, some of them already mentioned and many of them translated by our recurring John Mason Neale.

---

3   *The Hymns of the Breviary and Missal,* rev. ed. Matthew Britt (New York: Benziger Brothers, 1924), #55, p. 133.

Advent: The beloved "O Come, O Come, Emmanuel" (ELW 257 and LSB 357) stems from an early medieval collection of seven "O Antiphons" for the last week of Advent.[4] Neale here translated a late medieval Latin hymn that had put them together, as then adapted in subsequent English versions. For each day, a stanza invokes the coming Lord under biblical names such as Emmanuel, Branch of Jesse, or Key of David (Isaiah 7, 11, 22).

Christmas: "Lo, How a Rose E'er Blooming" (ELW 272 and LSB 359) is today a severe condensation of its original twenty-three stanzas in late medieval German. The shoot or branch, from Isaiah 11, was originally a reference to the Virgin Mary as the rose, but Protestant renditions have made sure that the hymn emphasizes "True man, yet very God" (st. 3).[5] A pre-Reformation hymn in the German language may sound rare, but there are many other examples. A mixture of Latin and German is the source for "Good Christian Friends, Rejoice" (ELW 288 and LSB 386), a medieval hymn from before 1400 and again one translated by John Mason Neale.[6]

Epiphany/Transfiguration: Also by Neale is an English translation of a fifteenth-century hymn for the Transfiguration at the end of the Epiphany season, namely, "Oh, Wondrous Image, Vision Fair" (ELW 316 and LSB 413). The tune, also from the fifteenth century, is perhaps more familiar as sung in "Oh, Love, How Deep," to be presented shortly. With Transfiguration Sunday, the season is about to turn to Lent on Ash Wednesday; so, the *Alleluia* is put aside until Easter, but not before a medieval hymn bids it farewell in "Alleluia, Song of Gladness" (ELW 318 and LSB 417), yet another of Neale's translations, albeit considerably altered.

---

4   For more on the "Great O" antiphons, see LSB 357 and the *LSB Companion* on that hymn.

5   For textual details, see *LSB Companion* 359, pp. 79–80.

6   For more on mixtures of German and Latin, see Anthony Ruff, "The Early Church and the Middle Ages," *LSB Companion*, vol. 2, 9–12.

Lent and Holy Week: "The Glory of These Forty Days" (ELW 320) extols the biblical and Lenten discipline of fasting, citing Moses, Elijah, Daniel, John, and Christ himself. Latin manuscripts from the eleventh century suggest that it was already in wide use then. For Palm Sunday, an earlier chapter has already presented Theodulf of Orléans back in the ninth century as well as John Mason Neale's keen interest in the story of his "All Glory, Laud, and Honor" (ELW 344 and LSB 442). Similarly, the Good Friday hymn "O Sacred Head, Now Wounded" (ELW 351 and LSB 449–50) has already been appreciated as a Latin medieval source for German and English versions.

Easter: As in other eras, hymns for Easter abounded in the late medieval context, too many to list here. Besides Fortunatus and John of Damascus as early medieval examples, see "At the Lamb's High Feast" (ELW 362 and LSB 633), full of biblical energy, and "That Easter Day with Joy Was Bright" (ELW 384), again translated by Neale. The classic "Jesus Christ is Risen Today" (ELW 365 and LSB 457) arose in the fourteenth century, originally in more stanzas but later blessed with a doxology (st. 4) added by Charles Wesley. A cluster of other late medieval Easter hymns was taken over by Martin Luther, as covered in the next chapter. Finally, Jean Tisserand (died in 1494) wrote a hymnic companion for Easter Day and the second Sunday of Easter, or St. Thomas Day, namely, "O Sons and Daughters, Let Us Sing" (ELW 386). Tisserand rounds out our medieval coverage of the Franciscan tradition, and this translation is one last credit to John Mason Neale.

Pentecost: With late medieval Pentecost hymns we come to a pattern that previews Martin Luther's contribution. "Now to the Holy Spirit Let Us Pray" (ELW 743 and LSB 768) takes its first stanza from a German song that was appreciated already in the thirteenth century. Luther liked it too and added three more stanzas. He did something similar for "Come, Holy Ghost, God and Lord" (ELW 395 and LSB 497), taking the first stanza from a German version of a medieval Latin antiphon for the Vigil of Pentecost and adding multiple stanzas of his own (LW 53: 265–267). As in these Pentecost examples, Luther's many hymns often began with brief existing hymn texts, whether Latin or German, and then he added his own stanzas to them.

That there were any German hymns at all before Martin Luther, not to mention German Bibles, may seem surprising. More on that shortly. But the late Middle Ages saw multiple hymns not only in Latin but also in the vernacular, the various languages of the people. Two Italian hymns, for example, can stand for others and introduce the idea of reforms in the Late Middle Ages.

Discendi, amor santo is well translated from Italian as "Come Down, O Love Divine" (ELW 804 and LSB 501). After Francis broke the ice with *Laudato Si,'* later spiritual movements in Italy featured other *laude spirituali* ("spiritual praises"), including works under that phrasing by Bianco da Siena (ca. 1350–1434). Representative of a lay movement, his extensive Italian poetry about Jesus and the Holy Spirit was translated by Richard F. Littledale, another friend of John Mason Neale. Of the several resulting hymns, this one is the best known, perhaps due in part to its pairing with a Ralph Vaughn Williams tune.

More dramatic and better known is the case of Girolamo Savonarola (1452–98), author of *Geisu sommo conforto* ("Jesus, Refuge of the Weary" LBW 93 and LSB 423). Savonarola's many works include his own *laude spirituali* as part of a broad critique of Florence's corrupt culture and the established church, too. He found local support at first, but then papal opposition. When his reforms and apocalyptic prophecies prompted excommunication in 1497, he defied the pope and urged Christian leaders to call a general council. In his case, the result was a heresy trial and execution in 1498, and it raises the larger issue of medieval reform movements and their outcomes—in other words, reforms before the Reformation.

Reforms Before the Reformation

Individual conversion stories sometimes exaggerate how ignorant and immoral the convert was before seeing the light. So too might some Protestants take false comfort in thinking that the Reformation saved Christianity from its captivity to a medieval church devoid of scripture, of grace, of Christ. The Benedictines alone, singing the Psalms all day every day, should correct the first charge, and St. Augustine as the teacher of grace is the obvious antidote to the second. Bernard of Clairvaux and Francis of Assisi had already testified to Christ and him crucified, but there is more. A century before the Reformation, "Oh, Love, How Deep, How Broad, How High" makes explicit what some today might think characteristic of the Protestant movement: Christ's work, "for us." But it must first be presented in the context of multiple reform movements in the Late Middle Ages. As the "new world" in 1492 was only new to Columbus and his crew, and not to its inhabitants, so too late medieval Christianity may surprise us with its multiple reform movements before the sixteenth-century Reformation.

Long before, an eleventh-century "Gregorian" reform named for Pope Gregory VII had reformed the standards for the education and celibacy of the clergy, plus freedom from the feudal lords. Bernard in the twelfth century and Francis, along with many others, were part of various movements to diversify and to reform monasticism. In Thomas Aquinas we saw how thirteenth-century scholasticism was itself a reform of schools and the teaching of theology. Fourteenth-century popular reformers like John Wycliffe (ca. 1330–84) in Oxford and then Jan Hus (ca. 1372–1415) in Prague had large followings. Certain of Wycliffe's philosophical theories generated trouble, for him and his followers, including some in Prague. Big councils in the fifteenth century attempted to reform the church by qualifying the power of the papacy. The Renaissance itself precedes the Reformation as a reform of the humanities (Humanism) as well as the arts.

Thomas à Kempis (ca. 1380–1471); "Oh, Love, How Deep" (ELW 322, LSB 544)

Thomas à Kempis

One particular reform movement frames the story of this hymn: the "New Devotion" (*Devotio Moderna*) associated with Thomas à Kempis and *The Imitation of Christ*. Like Francis before him, Geert Groote (1340–84) renounced his life of Dutch wealth and resolved to live simply and devoutly, in this case leading to communities not bound by vows or organized into an order. They became known as the "Brethren of the Common Life," and one such community in Holland shaped Thomas from Kempen (ca. 1380–1471). His long career as a scribe, writer, preacher, and spiritual advisor is summed up in *The Imitation of Christ*, a classic of devotional literature widely copied and then often printed in the fifteenth century. Like the hymn text, this famous work is credited to Thomas without definitive proof, but both are clearly expressive of his views and his community. "Christ is ready to come to you, with what kindness in his glance! . . . Up with you, then, faithful soul, get your heart ready for the coming of this true Lover. . . . Ah,

Oh, Love, How Deep

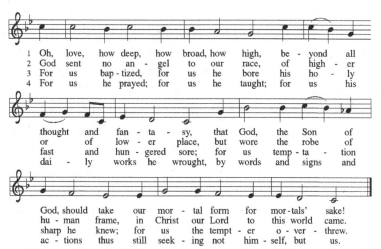

1 Oh, love, how deep, how broad, how high, be - yond all thought and fan - ta - sy, that God, the Son of God, should take our mor - tal form for mor-tals' sake!

2 God sent no an - gel to our race, of high - er or of low - er place, but wore the robe of hu - man frame, in Christ our Lord to this world came.

3 For us bap - tized, for us he bore his ho - ly fast and hun - gered sore; for us temp - ta - tion sharp he knew; for us the tempt - er o - ver - threw.

4 For us he prayed; for us he taught; for us his dai - ly works he wrought, by words and signs and ac - tions thus still seek - ing not him - self, but us.

5 For us by wickedness betrayed,
for us, in crown of thorns arrayed,
he bore the shameful cross and death;
for us he gave his dying breath.

6 For us he rose from death again;
for us he went on high to reign;
for us he sent his Spirit here
to guide, to strengthen, and to cheer.

7 All glory to our Lord and God
for love so deep, so high, so broad:
the Trinity whom we adore
forever and forevermore.

Text: Thomas á Kempis, 1380–1471; tr. Benjamin Webb, 1819–1885, alt.
Music: DEO GRACIAS, English ballad, 15th cent.

but it is above your reach (you complain), such high contemplation of heavenly things. Why then, let your mind come to rest in Christ's passion, and find in his sacred wounds the home it longs for."[7] The book circulated since 1418, with extant manuscripts since 1441, and was first printed in 1471 and dozens of times before 1500, making it one of the earliest and most often printed books after the Bible in the cradle years of printing. All this testifies to the market for the new devotion.

---

7 Thomas à Kempis, *Imitation of Christ,* Book II, chapter 1, as cited in Hugh Kerr, *Readings in Christian Thought,* 2nd edition (Nashville: Abingdon Press, 1990), 132–133.

The hymn "Oh, Love, How Deep" also expresses these Bernardine sentiments, with a special refrain: "for us." But the stanzas we sing are only a small portion of the original poem. Benjamin Webb (1819–85), another contemporary of John Mason Neale, translated only a handful of the twenty-three stanzas. His first line paraphrases *O amor quam exstaticus* ("O love, how ecstatic") with spatial qualities of deep, broad, and high, since "ecstasy" had lost its original meaning of going outside oneself as God did in becoming human. The second stanza, originally the fourth, starts a sequence (originally stanzas 4–8) about Jesus's incarnation, manger, circumcision and naming, and thirty years as a human among humans, all for us. The original stanza nine, our third, begins a section dominated by *nobis*; "for us" baptized, tempted, betrayed, whipped, spat upon, and crucified. "For us by wickedness betrayed, for us in crown of thorns arrayed, he bore the shameful cross and death; for us he gave his dying breath" (ELW 322, st. 5). After the resurrection and ascension, again "for us," the original poem extols such love at length, coming back around to Bethlehem in the last verses. It was originally a Christmas composition regarding the extent of God's love in the incarnation (Titus 3:4) all the way to death and resurrection. Webb, however, in choosing the central "passion" portion, made it a modern Lenten hymn. His translation has been adapted over time and a different doxology has replaced his original, and accurate, translation about such boundless love. "To him whose boundless love has won salvation for us through his Son, to God the Father, glory be both now and through eternity."[8]

Even the tune is pre-Reformation, stemming from a widely used ballad called DEO GRACIAS and associated with King Henry V's victory at the 1415 Battle of Agincourt in the Hundred Years War. "Oh, Wondrous Image, Vision Fair" (ELW 316), sung to the same tune, is based on a different text but one that is also from the fifteenth century.

---

8   Routley-Richardson, *Panorama*, #167B, p. 161.

Jan Hus and Czech Hymnody

IAN HVS,
voorgangher van Luther, is inde Stadt Con:
stans Levendigh Verbrandt,

Jan Hus

Perhaps the best example of "reforms before the Reformation" and of a specific reformer is the late medieval Bohemian movement around Prague and the career of the professor-preacher Jan Hus (ca. 1370–1415). This Czech reform movement preceded Hus, and it diversified and flourished after him, in part because of his work and martyr's fame. Into this short space we must compress the larger story of the career of Hus himself, whose legacy features hymns at key points.

Hus was born around 1370 in the southern Bohemian village of Husinec. He called himself Jan of Husinec at first, but the short form is what stuck. By 1390 he was a student at the University of Prague where he stayed for his whole teaching and preaching career until its tragic end. Around 1402 Hus was not only the dean of the University's Faculty of Arts but also the rector-preacher at Prague's independent Bethlehem Chapel, founded in 1391 by the Bohemian reformers especially for preaching in Czech. Hus's decade in this role led to great influence, for he preached daily to large crowds, indeed sometimes to the chapel's full capacity of three thousand hearers. In lectures, sermons, and books, Hus advocated for reforms that would echo a century later in Protestant Germany. He criticized greedy and immoral clergy, he scolded lay pilgrims for flocking to superstitious sites, and he stoutly condemned superficial indulgences in Luther-like terms. Instead of buying an indulgent (easy) way around penance, they both said that Christians should thoroughly repent and turn their lives around. Further, this movement became famous for distributing communion for all in both bread and wine, with frequent reception by the laity.

To our theme, hymns and songs played a large role in the Bohemian movement overall, in Hus's own life, and in his afterlife as a heroic figure. As seen already in German and other vernaculars, hymns in Czech were known and often sung before Hus, and he had some of them depicted on the walls of the Bethlehem Chapel. Hus led such hymns, commended them, and became known for a few of his own.

Hus got into trouble with his archbishop for several reasons, including defending some of Wycliffe's Oxford teachings and appealing to Christ above the pope and to scriptural truth above Roman Catholic rules. The archbishop told him to stop preaching, but he would not. After a long process, he was summoned to the general church council in Constance, imprisoned there, tried, and convicted as a heretic without much chance to defend himself. He was burned at the stake near the Rhine on July 6, 1415. By Czech tradition he went to the flames singing hymns, and his followers naturally wrote songs about him thereafter as their hero.

As with other famous figures, devoted disciples later incorrectly attributed to him various Bohemian hymns, but by all accounts he did write a few himself. Some careful studies identify a handful of hymns by Hus, most of them not in common use, but even these attributions are still debated, including one that has considerable evidence, namely,

"Jesus Christ, Our God and Savior"
WALTER 1524

1. Je - sus Christ, our God and Sav - ior,

Turned a - way God's wrath for ev - - - er,

By his bit - ter ag - o - ny

Helped us out of hell's mis - - er - y.

2 That we never should forget it
Gave he us his flesh to eat it,
Hidden in this bit of bread,
And to drink gave us his blood.

3 Whoso to this board repaireth,
Take good heed how he prepareth.
Who unworthy thither goes,
Thence death instead of life he knows.

4 God the Father praise thou duly,
That he thee would feed so truly,
And for ill deeds by thee done
Up unto death has given his Son.

5 Have this faith, and do not waver,
'Tis food for every craver
Who, his heart with sin opprest,
Can no more for its anguish rest.

6 Such kindness and such grace to get,
Seeks a heart with agony great.
Is it well with thee? take care,
Lest at last thou shouldst evil fare.

7 Lo, he saith himself, "Ye weary
Come to me and I will cheer ye;
Needless were the doctor's skill
To the souls that be strong and well.

8 "Hadst thou any claim to proffer,
Why for thee then should I suffer?
This table is not for thee,
If thou wilt set thine own self free."

9 If such faith thy heart possesses,
And the same thy mouth confesses,
Fit guest then thou art indeed,
And this food thine own soul will feed.

10 Fruit of faith therein be showing
That thou art to others loving;
To thy neighbor thou wilt do
As God in love hath done to you.

Luther's Works 53: 250-251 (Fortress Press, 1965)

his expansion (to twenty-one stanzas) of "Jesus Christ, O Munificent Priest."[9] The best-known hymn associated with Hus was perhaps not by him at all, and in any case was wholly rewritten by Martin Luther: "Jesus Christ, Our Blessed Savior" (LSB 627, LW 53: 250–251). The original hymn, known from a Latin manuscript in 1410 and then in Czech, celebrates the sacrament as befitted the Bohemian encouragement to appreciate it and receive it often. Luther retained only the first few words and went on to pen "essentially a new hymn" with his distinctive emphases on Christ's gift to be received in humble faith and then expressed in love for the neighbor.[10] See especially stanzas 8 and 10.

It became Luther's own, appeared in the earliest Evangelical hymnals in 1524, and was widely used thereafter as a Lutheran communion hymn. Luther's header kept alive his predecessor's name, and indeed even gave him the title of saint, although the attribution was later regarded as doubtful: "The Hymn of St. Jan Huss, Improved."

Luther was well aware of Hus's career and had to endure critics like John Eck insisting that he was just another heretic like Hus. At one point, paying tribute to his Bohemian forerunner, Luther said of himself and his circle "we are all Hussites without knowing it" (LW 48: 153). Also on a musical note, Luther repeated a fanciful prophecy attributed to Hus, whose name meant "goose." Near the stake, Hus supposedly said "Now they roast a goose but in a hundred years they shall hear a swan sing, whom they will not be able to do away with" (LW 34: 103).

---

9   For an overview on Hus and hymnody, see David Holeton and Hana Vlhorá-Wörner, "The Second Life of Jan Hus: Liturgy, Commemoration, Music," *A Companion to Jan Hus*, ed. F. Šmohel (Leiden: Brill, 2015), esp. 291–301, with this hymn text at 322–324.

10   Robin Leaver, "Jesus Christus unser Heiland," *Luther's Liturgical Music* (Grand Rapids, MI: Eerdmans, 2007), 156. To be cited as Leaver, *Luther's Liturgical Music*. See the *LSB Companion* 627 for a discussion of authorship. There is a recent and partial (5 stanzas) translation in *All Creation Sings* 963.

Apart from Reformation hymn texts and some legendary comments, there are also songs from the Bohemian Brethren that have lived on in modern hymnals, such as a late fifteenth-century Czech Christmas carol ("Let Our Gladness Have No End," ELW 291 and LSB 381), and the lively tunes of "At the Lamb's High Feast We Sing" (ELW 362 and LSB 633, also used in ELW 657) and "Come, You Faithful, Raise the Strain" of John of Damascus (ELW 363 and LSB 487). The career and the fate of Jan Hus nicely demonstrate the general late medieval theme of reforms before the Reformation.

Coda

Before leaving the vast topic of medieval texts that have become hymns, three chapters' worth, we should remember that throughout the Middle Ages the texts most often sung in church were not hymns in the modern sense but specific biblical passages intoned in liturgical contexts. First, in the Mass the "Ordinary" was mostly sung Scripture: the *Kyrie,* the *Gloria,* the biblical message of the *Credo,* the *Alleluia* (except in Lent), the *Sanctus/Benedictus,* and the *Agnus Dei.* Further in the Mass, variable Propers such as the Introit and Gradual were also sung scripture, albeit not hymns. Today, these Latin texts are more familiar in classical music, with compositions galore. Second, the daily prayers of countless monastic communities were dominated by singing the Psalms, plus other biblical canticles, along with the *Gloria Patri,* the *Te Deum,* and some "Ambrosian" hymns.

7

MARTIN LUTHER AND THE REFORMATION (1500–1600)

"A New Song"

MARTIN LUTHER (1483–1546) played a pivotal role in the history of hymn texts, although his work built upon previous generations and was shared with key colleagues in his own time. The myth of Luther single-handedly creating the first German hymns for congregational singing, as well as the first German Bible, cannot survive the evidence of prior texts such as the late medieval Hussite songs just mentioned. There were previous German Bibles too, although they were not translated from the Greek and Hebrew. Luther's creative use of German had important precedents, and he took over some of them in the hymns he appropriated. Many of his hymns start with texts he inherited, whether from Scripture or from

Martin Luther

church history. His original hymns, especially "Dear Christians, One and All, Rejoice," reflect his own experience quite personally.

The quincentennial of Lutheran hymnals (1524–2024) now provides some context, for apart from some small Hussite collections they were the first congregational hymnbooks in all of Christian history.[1] Monastic communities had a form of hymnal for their members, but the new Lutheran hymnals were intended for parish use and at home.

Overall, Luther's distinctive concern was for the reform of worship, and especially to communicate that the Lord's Supper was not our sacrifice to God but God's sacramental gift to us, the good-news gospel of "given for you, for the forgiveness of sins" (Matthew 26:28). For this message to be heard, such proclamation in Scripture, sermon, liturgy, and hymnody needed to be in the everyday language of the people. For Luther, hymns were not primarily prayer, but instruction and especially proclamation, like sermons. The main thing to appreciate about Luther's overall reform movement is how devoted it was to the effective transmission of the inherited message of Scripture. The gospel was conveyed to him, and then by him, through the biblical readings and the liturgical texts of worship, in the traditional catechism, and in hymns. This means both prior hymns, whether ancient or recent, and also hymns newly created by Luther and his team.

Luther's musical activities are well-known, not only singing and playing the lute, but also arranging and composing the music for some hymns, canticles, and the liturgy. Just as he translated and adapted traditional texts, so he also simplified and arranged some inherited melodies for congregational singing. With the help of the musician Johann Walter (1496–1570) and others, the first "Evangelical" hymnbooks in 1524–26 give ample testimony to the musical side of Luther's contribution to Reformation hymnody.[2] As for posterity, later giants like J. S.

---

1   Robin Leaver, editor, *A New Song We Now Begin: Celebrating the Half Millennium of Lutheran Hymnals (1524–2024)* (Minneapolis: Fortress Press, 2024).

2   On Luther's musical talents, see Leaver, *Luther's Liturgical Music,* chapter 2. For Luther's own hymns, see *Luther's Works,* vol. 53, cited as LW 53.

Bach and F. Mendelssohn honored Luther's original compositions with cantatas and arrangements of his work, such as his expressive melody for Psalm 130 *Aus tiefer Not* ("Out of the Depths," ELW 600). Further, the sheer staying power of Luther's melodies today in congregational song worldwide is its own testimony to his musical contribution. His tributes to music as one of God's greatest gifts indicate yet another aspect of the topic that is impossible to cover here. Clearly, Luther had musical gifts, but our attention must stay on the texts, both the many inherited texts he translated, paraphrased, and proclaimed, and also the few new hymn texts he wrote.

Luther's Array of Inherited Hymn Texts

The first challenge in presenting Luther's hymn texts is their sheer quantity and variety. Even more than Ambrose before him, the Wittenberg professor was a prolific hymn-writer. The American Edition of *Luther's Works* (vol 53) lists thirty-seven hymns, and there is still more material forthcoming. They could be organized topically, as most hymnals do regarding the church year and an array of themes, or chronologically, as in the volume of *Luther's Works,* thereby showing that fully two-thirds of Luther's hymns were produced in 1523–24. But our focus on the cumulative history of hymn texts over the centuries suggests another approach.

Thinking historically, we can distinguish the prior texts that Luther used and adapted, whether out of Scripture or the tradition, from his newly written hymn texts. The numerous inherited texts fall into four groups: first, biblical texts such as the Psalms; second, biblical-liturgical passages used in the Mass, such as the *Gloria* or *Sanctus*; third, biblical-catechetical texts such as the Ten Commandments and the Lord's Prayer; and fourth, early and medieval texts such as those by Ambrose and the medieval hymns mentioned in the previous section.

Biblical

Luther was famously the first to translate the New Testament from Greek into German, a project undertaken during a few months of enforced retreat in 1521. Then, with a team of colleagues, he translated the Old Testament from Hebrew into German and published the whole "Luther Bible" in 1534, complete with introductions, illustrations, and marginal notes. There had been other German translations of the Bible, but they were produced from the Latin version. Plus, Luther's rendition featured such effective, down-to-earth wording that it quickly dominated the field and even influenced the German language. Every translation involves some interpretation, and Luther's emphasis on grace and faith led to some controversial choices, such as adding "alone" to Romans 3:28: "justified by faith *alone.*"

When Luther also paraphrased the Psalms and other biblical canticles to make them singable for congregational use, he, like many others after him, did not hesitate to give them a Christian interpretation—sometimes explicitly. Early on he recruited colleagues to help with such Psalms and German hymns in general, as indicated in his 1523 comments on public worship and in his correspondence. He encouraged "any German poets to compose evangelical hymns for us," and he explained that new translations should not cling to every word but use free language, even paraphrases, to get the message across.[3] He led the way with his own version of Psalm 130, "Out of the Depths I Cry to Thee," adding an emphasis on unmerited grace (ELW 600, with the five-stanza version in LSB 607), as mentioned already. Psalm 12 became "Ah God, from Heaven Look Down" (LW 53: 225), and Psalm 14 became "Although the Fools Say with Their Mouth" (LW 53: 229) with mention of "Christ his Son." Psalm 67 became "Would That the Lord Would Grant Us Grace" (LW 53: 232, LSB 823–24), with Father, Son, and Holy Ghost in stanza 3. Psalm 124 became "Were God Not with Us at This Time" (LW 53: 245), and Psalm 128 became "Happy who in God's Fear Doth Stay" (LW 53: 242). These Psalms were naturally used for Matins and Vespers in the 1524–25 orders of worship, as monastics had been using Latin Psalms

---

3   Quoting LW 53: 37; with LW 49: 68–69 and LW 53: 221.

for centuries. Further, he provided a singable version of Simeon's *Nunc dimittis*, "Lord, Now Let Your Servant Depart in Peace," also used in worship ("In Peace and Joy," ELW 440, LBW 528, LSB 938). As with the Psalms, other biblical canticles were also arranged for congregational use by Luther and his team of colleagues, such as the *Magnificat* (LW 53: 176–79). These Psalms and canticles were meant to be sung in worship, not only by a choir but also by the congregation.

Biblical-Liturgical

Secondly, the liturgy gave Luther some other biblical texts to translate into singable form, including in the "German Mass" in 1526. The *Kyrie* ("Lord, have mercy") naturally appeared in several places. One German paraphrase of the *Gloria in excelsis* was written by Luther's colleague Nicolaus Decius (LBW 166, ELW 410, LSB 947; more on him below) but another translation may have been written by Luther himself (LW 53: 184–88, LSB 948). For the *Credo*, not quoting from Scripture but summarizing its message, see the next section on catechetical hymns. For the *Sanctus*, Luther cited Isaiah 6:1–4 in full: "Isaiah in a Vision Did of Old" (LW 53: 82–83, ELW 868, LSB 960). Finally, the *Agnus Dei* became a German "Lamb of God" (LW 53: 151–52), if not by Luther, then by one of his partners in this overall endeavor to render the communion liturgy in German.

Biblical-Catechetical

Third, Luther's hymns were catechetical, both in general as means of instruction and also more specifically as presenting the components of the traditional catechism. In fact, Luther's *Small Catechism* was sometimes printed with hymns included for specific sections. The 1543 Wittenberg hymnal grouped the catechetical hymns together. For example, the 1524 "These Are the Holy Ten Commands" (LSB 581, LW 53: 277–79) puts the biblical Decalogue in a singable form. See also Luther's shorter hymn on the Decalogue: "Man, Wouldst Thou Live All Blissfully" (LW 53: 280–81). For the creed, Luther reworked an earlier German version that had combined parts of the Apostles' Creed and the Nicene Creed, resulting in "We All Believe in One True God" (ELW 411, LSB 954, LW 53: 271–73). "The Lord's Prayer" became "Our Father, God in Heaven Above" (ELW 746–47, LSB 766).

For catechesis on the sacraments, Luther's hymns drew on the scriptural scenes of Jesus's baptism and the Last Supper. In 1540–41, paraphrasing Luke 3 and Matthew 28, Luther wrote "To Jordan Came the Christ, Our Lord" (LSB 406–407, LBW 79, LW 53: 299–301). Similarly, the Lord's Supper was the subject of Luther's musical attention in several ways. Just as his Small Catechism emphasized Jesus's words "given for you, . . . for the forgiveness of sins," so his instructions for the liturgy stipulated that the Last Supper account (the biblical *Verba*, or Words of Institution) should be chanted in the same tone as the Gospel lesson, as proclaiming the good news in a distilled form (LW 53: 56). One of the hymns that Luther commended in his "German Mass" for singing during communion was also catechetical, namely, the long hymn he thought was by the fifteenth-century Czech reformer Jan Hus discussed earlier, namely, "Jesus Christ, Our Blessed Savior" (ACS 963, LSB 627). With its advocacy of communion in bread and wine, and as proclamation of grace "for you," this hymn was particularly fitting for catechetical use.[4]

Early and Medieval Sources

Fourth, and already previewed, Luther received and adapted texts from the early and medieval church. Some of these were his German adaptations of full hymns, such as "Savior of the Nations, Come" by Ambrose. Luther also translated a brief hymn for Vespers that he thought was by Ambrose but remains anonymous: "Thou Who Art Three in Unity"

4　For Luther's "musical catechesis" in all these hymns, see Leaver, *Luther's Liturgical Music*, chapters 4–11. For the communion hymns, see LW 53: 82; LSB 627; LW 53: 249–251; see also the shortened version of the "Hus" hymn in *All Creation Sings* 963, by Martin A. Seltz and Paul Westermeyer. For another communion hymn, "O Lord We Praise You" (ELW 499) with roots in late medieval singing, see the next section.

(LW 53: 308–09, from *O Lux beata Trinitas*, Walsh, *Hymns* #49). From one poem by the fifth-century Sedulius (*A solis ortus cardine*, Walsh, *Hymns* #19) came two traditional Latin Christmas-Epiphany hymns that Luther translated as "Jesus We Now Must Laud and Sing" (LW 53: 237–39) and "Herod, Why Dreadest Thou" (LW 53: 302–03). As mentioned earlier, Luther translated two Latin classics: the *Te Deum* (LW 53: 171–75) and Rhabanus Maurus's "Come, God Creator Holy Ghost" (LW 53: 260; ELW 577–78). The Hus communion hymn just mentioned also shows Luther's freedom in paraphrasing a hymn from church history.

Luther also reused several late medieval anonymous hymns, many of them in German, with a striking strategy.[5] Starting with a known tune and text for the first stanza, Luther would add his own texts for subsequent stanzas, meaning that the congregation would have a familiar start but then receive a new message. We have already seen examples from Pentecost hymns (ELW 395 and 743, LSB 768). Luther did something similar for a Christmas hymn, "All Praise to You" (LSB 382 with further details in the LSB *Companion*; LBW 48; LW 53: 240–41) and turned a Marian hymn into a triune invocation ("Triune God, Be Thou Our Stay," LSB 505; "God the Father With Us Be," LW 53: 268–70; LBW 308). The popular medieval cry for help *Media Vita* became "Even as We Live Each Day" (LBW 350) with Luther's two additional verses invoking the atoning blood and the forgiveness of sin (LW 53: 274–76, LSB 755, *All Creation Sings* 1026).

Two more examples round out Luther's adaptation of prior texts. Luther reused both the text and the tune of a popular late medieval German communion song as stanza 1 of "O Lord We Praise You." Then the congregations (also in "Reformed" Strasbourg!) would go on to sing Luther's next two stanzas including the fruits of the sacramental gift (LW 53: 252–54, ELW 499, LSB 617). Luther's great Easter hymn

---

5 For a separate confirmation that Luther's movement used existing German hymns, see P. Melanchthon's *Apology* 24.4, *The Book of Concord*, ed. R. Kolb and T. Wengert (Minneapolis: Fortress Press, 2000), 258.

"Christ Jesus Lay in Death's Strong Bands" (ELW 370, LSB 458) has an even fuller medieval background. An eleventh-century Easter "sequence" text in Latin attributed to one Wipo of Burgundy (ELW 371) was sometimes paired with a twelfth-century hymn in German that was popular in Luther's time ("Christ is Arisen" ELW 372). He adjusted the tune for his own powerful seven-stanza proclamation of the passion and resurrection of Christ (LSB 458, LW 53: 255–57). Dead center in the hymn is the "strange and dreadful strife when life and death contended" (LSB 458, st. 4), as J. S. Bach's Cantata 4 features so powerfully, but this symmetry is lost in the truncated versions (LBW 134, ELW 370).[6]

All in all, Luther's "inherited" hymn texts reveal two important patterns. First, they are clearly more numerous than his newly composed hymn texts. For an example from current usage, *Evangelical Lutheran Worship* has fifteen "Luther hymns" (texts), with seven of them inherited fully, four of them mixed (such as the first stanza from the tradition), and four are newly written. The proportions are similar in the larger array of Luther hymns in the *Lutheran Service Book* hymnal, and in the full list in *Luther's Works,* volume 53. Second, Luther did not just pass along these received texts in mere translations, but rather adapted and often expanded them to reflect his own expression of the biblical message. In fact, this pattern of using the tradition even applies to the so-called newly written hymns coming into view.

New Hymns

Of Luther's few original hymn texts, three are well-known and from relatively late in his career. First, from the late 1520s comes the classic "Mighty Fortress," a hymn-sermon that engages a few phrases of Psalm 46. Its text and music have been analyzed carefully, including the

---

6   See also "Grant Peace, We Pray," an early medieval Latin antiphon translated by Luther; ELW 784, LSB 777–78, LW 53: 286–287.

convoluted history of English translations.[7] Second, once Luther had a family of his own, he paraphrased the Lukan angel's message sometime in the early 1530s, and added responses for children of all ages. In J. Klug's 1535 hymnal, the result was called a "Children's Hymn for Christmas Eve," namely, "From Heaven Above to Earth I Come," using the pattern of a folk song for the opening words (ELW 268, LSB 358). Third, in the early 1540s, Luther wrote a wholly new text in three short trinitarian stanzas: "Lord, Keep Us Steadfast in Your Word" (ELW 517, LSB 655). Amid the military advances of the "Counter Reformation" papacy and the Islamic forces from Istanbul nearing Vienna, Luther's second line made sense at the time ("and curb the Turks' and papists' sword," LW 53: 305), but it was replaced early on by more irenic phrasing.

As widespread in usage as these three later hymns became, the best way to appreciate Luther's innovative place in the history of hymn texts is to look more closely at his first products. In Luther's time, news in general was sometimes spread by singing a ballad, such as Meistersinger Hans Sachs's 1523 folk song about the Reformer himself as the "Wittenberg Nightingale."[8] For Luther's first song, he wrote a ballad of his own that same year, conveying and interpreting the sad news that some young Augustinian friars had been burned at the stake in Brussels on July 1, 1523, for the heresy of his own teachings. Amid Luther's anguish at their ordeal, the text celebrates their defiance of those responsible. Called "A New Song Here Shall Be Begun" (LW 53: 211–16), it was also indicative of the outpouring of more new songs from Luther and his cohorts.[9]

---

7   For example, see Andreas Loewe and Katherine Firth, "Martin Luther's 'Mighty Fortress,'" *Lutheran Quarterly* 32 (2018): 125–145. On the English translations, see Westermeyer, *ELW Companion* 503, as also glimpsed in the comparative translations in ELW 503 and 505 or in LSB 656–57 with Spanish too.

8   For links between Sachs and Luther's own ballad, see Robin Leaver, *The Whole Church Sings* (Grand Rapids, MI: Eerdmans, 2017), 55–63.

9   See Robert Christman, "The Antwerp Martyrs and Luther's First Song," *Lutheran Quarterly* 36 (2022): 373–389.

"Dear Christians, One and All, Rejoice"
(ELW 594, LSB 556)

Luther's second song in 1523, *Nun freut euch,* known as "Dear Christians, One and All, Rejoice," starts off with echoes of a familiar song in text and tune, the pattern we have noted in so many of his other hymns. (See LSB 556 and LBW 299 for all ten stanzas, also in LW 53: 217–20; ELW 594 has eight stanzas). But then it is wholly Luther's own account, and mirrors his own story. In theme and structure, it narrates salvation itself, as captured by its header in a 1533 Wittenberg hymnal: "How a Sinner Comes to Grace."[10] The opening stanza calls all Christians to rejoice and sing: God's wonders for us mean victory, but at a cost. Atonement is here presented not as a theological theory, but in a homiletical narration of events that are unfolding now and applied to us, both individually and collectively. First, the plight of the sinner; then, how the sinner comes to grace. The second stanza itemizes Satan, death, and sin as overpowering. Then comes more bad news. "My own good works all came to naught, No grace or merit gaining; Free will against God's judgment fought, Dead to all good remaining. My fears increased till sheer despair Left only death to be my share; The pangs of hell I suffered" (LBW 299 st. 3, LSB 556, st. 3). Even good works and free will, much on Luther's mind in his debate with Erasmus around that time, are no help. Sheer despair, death, and hell prevail. Alas, the *Evangelical Lutheran Worship* version drops part of this section, compressing two stanzas into one and thereby softening the grim predicament.

The narrative then shifts to God's perspective, who mercifully saw "my deep distress" and "turned to me a father's heart" (ELW 594, st. 3). Here the first-person singular pronouns can stand for Luther's own experience of grace, and also for any individual who sings these lines. A generation later, a Lutheran observer marveled that this very

---

10   Leaver, *Luther's Liturgical Music,* 163–165.

Dear Christians, One and All, Rejoice

1 Dear Chris-tians, one and all, re-joice, with ex-ul-ta-tion
2 Fast bound in Sa-tan's chains I lay, death brood-ed fierce-ly
3 O God, you saw my deep dis-tress be-fore the world's foun-
4 You said to your be-lov-ed Son: "'Tis time to have com-

spring-ing, and, with u-nit-ed heart and voice and ho-ly
o'er me, sin was my tor-ment night and day; in sin my
da-tion, and, with your mer-cy mea-sure-less, you planned for
pas-sion. Then go, bright jew-el of my crown, and bring to

rap-ture sing-ing, pro-claim the won-ders God has done, pro-
moth-er bore me. My own good works all came to naught, free
my sal-va-tion. You turned to me a fa-ther's heart; you
all sal-va-tion; from sin and sor-row set them free; slay

claim the vic-t'ry God has won, how pre-cious was our ran-som!
will a-gainst God's judg-ment fought, so firm-ly sin pos-sessed me.
did not choose the eas-y part, but gave your dear-est trea-sure.
bit-ter death for them that they may live with you for-ev-er."

5 The Son obeyed your gracious will,
was born of virgin mother;
and, your good pleasure to fulfill,
he came to be my brother.
His royal pow'r disguised he bore,
a servant's form, like mine, he wore,
to lead the devil captive.

6 To me he said: "Stay close to me,
I am your rock and castle.
Your ransom I myself will be;
for you I strive and wrestle.
The foe will shed my precious blood;
all this I suffer for your good;
my life o'er death will triumph.

7 "Now to my Father I depart,
from earth to heav'n ascending,
and, gracious wisdom to impart,
the Holy Spirit sending,
who will in trouble comfort you,
will teach you well, your faith renew,
and in all truth will guide you.

8 "What I on earth have done and taught
guide all your life and teaching;
so shall the glorious reign of God
increase, the whole world reaching.
Let none the gospel gift impede;
I make you free; be free indeed!
This final word I leave you."

Text: Martin Luther, 1483–1546; tr. hymnal version
Music: NUN FREUT EUCH, *Etlich christlich Lieder*, Wittenberg, 1524
Text © 2006 Augsburg Fortress.

hymn had led "many hundreds . . . to faith."[11] With the next stanza the hymn turns trinitarian, not in the abstract but in the saving events. God tells his Son, his dearest treasure, to "bring to all salvation . . . that they may live with you forever," and the Son later sends the Holy Spirit to comfort, teach, and guide. God's self-expression in the Son is born a servant and "my brother." In ELW 594 stanza 6, Christ's "ransom" line is, literally, "I give myself all up for thee" (see MacDonald's translation in LW 53: 220), a uniting that becomes mutual: "For I am yours, and you are Mine."

Here Luther has tapped the long tradition of using marital union to describe union with Christ, stemming from Ephesians 5 along with Hosea 2, as noted in Bernard of Clairvaux's poetic exposition of the Song of Songs. In fact, this very dialogue between Christ and the soul, "I am yours and you are mine" as adapted from Song of Songs 2:16, was common coin in late medieval spiritual writing, as Luther also knew from his mentor Johannes von Staupitz.[12] Luther's own influential 1520 treatise *The Freedom of the Christian* was eloquent on the subject, where he shifts the focus from love to faith. "The third incomparable benefit of faith is that it unites the soul with Christ as a bride is united with her bridegroom. By this mystery, as the Apostle teaches, Christ and the soul become one flesh" (LW 31: 351). This "happy exchange" motif, also invoking 2 Corinthians 5, became a well-known part of Luther's message, and the marital motif shows up often in later Lutheran hymnody.[13] Here too, unfortunately, the version in

---

11   C. Boyd Brown, *Singing the Gospel: Lutheran Hymns and the Success of the Reformation* (Cambridge, MA: Harvard University Press, 2005), 16, quoting T. Heshusius in 1555.

12   See Berndt Hamm, *The Early Luther: Stages in a Reformation Reorientation* (Grand Rapids, MI: Eerdmans, 2014), 208, for the fuller Staupitz quotation.

13   Besides Philipp Nicolai, Johann Franck, and Lina Sandell in the next chapter, see also J. Walter's "The Bridegroom Soon Will Call Us" (LSB 514), L. Laurenti's "Rejoice, Rejoice, Believers" (ELW 244), and Nikolaus Herman's "Let All Together Praise Our God" (ELW 287, st. 5; LSB 389, st. 4).

Evangelical Lutheran Worship compresses too much. Its conflation of stanzas 7–8 into one omits these lines of sheer gospel, "I am yours and you are Mine" (LBW 299, st. 7, LSB 556, st. 7) just as it earlier abbreviated the full disaster of sin.

In conclusion, death and resurrection are quickly narrated, not as in the distant past but as happening now, for our blessing. "Though he [the foe] will shed My precious blood, Of life me thus bereaving, All this I suffer for your good; Be steadfast and believing. Life will from death the vict'ry win; My innocence shall bear your sin. And you are blest forever" (LBW 299, st. 8, LSB 556, st. 8). The full text reads like a sermonic retelling of Romans 1–8, also pivotal for Luther's thought as to how the sinner comes to grace. It was "preaching in song."[14] No wonder that *Nun freut euch* became a standard pulpit hymn, next to the Creed and sermon, providing an exposition of "law and gospel," as Luther's theme became known. It was the very first hymn in those first 1524 hymnals and in many German hymnals thereafter. Philipp Nicolai quotes fully seven of its stanzas in his 1599 *Mirror.*

Luther's Partners in Hymnody

Luther was not alone in providing hymns for evangelical singing. Indeed, one such partner wrote three of the first eight collected hymns in the 1524 *Achtliederbuch*, namely, the learned Paul Speratus (1484–1551). One of them is an enduring "law and gospel" classic, originally in fourteen stanzas: "Salvation Unto Us Has Come" (LSB 555). Besides Speratus, Luther's early collaborators included Nikolaus Decius (1485–1550), a Benedictine monk with musical gifts who became Luther's Wittenberg student in 1523. His words and music for the *Agnus Dei* are still in use ("Lamb of God," LBW 111, ELW 357, LSB 434) and his paraphrase of the *Gloria in excelsis* became and remains the standard hymn version in German and

---

14   *Sonora praedicatio*, LW 53: 316 and 323; LW 54: 129.

English ("All Glory Be to God on High," LBW 155, ELW 410, LSB 947). Further on the musical side was Johann Walter (1496–1570), the composer and cantor who worked closely with Luther, especially for the choral versions of his hymns.[15] His 1524 "Choir Song Book" was formative for the Lutheran musical tradition. After the Hussite forerunners, these Lutheran hymnals could be considered the first Christian hymnals, at least in the sense of congregational song books, since previous collections were for monastic use. As the Lutheran Reformation unfolded through the sixteenth century and as its hymnals proliferated for use in church and home, many others contributed to this hymnody, but one early name stands out from the roster of men: Elisabeth.

Elisabeth Cruciger; "The Only Son from Heaven" (ELW 309, LSB 402)

When Luther put out his call for translations and new hymns in German, one answer came from a former nun who had fled her convent to live in Wittenberg. Like Katherina von Bora, who became her neighbor and friend, Elisabeth von Meseritz (ca. 1500–35) married an evangelical theologian, Wittenberg student Caspar Cruciger, and together they frequented Luther's table. Luther once said, "Everywhere we are looking for poets," and Elisabeth responded with *Herr Christ, der einig Gotts Sohn*, known today as "The Only Son from Heaven" (LBW 86, ELW 309, LSB 402). It was immediately included in some of the earliest Lutheran hymnals of 1524 (Erfurt and Walter's *Gesangbuch*), and regularly thereafter. Throughout the sixteenth century it appeared under her name in several hymnals, including translations into Swedish (Olaf Petri, 1520s) and English (Miles Coverdale, 1535). However, in later centuries scholars often attributed it not to her but,

---

15   For more on Walter, see W. Buszin, "Walter, Johann," *The Encyclopedia of the Lutheran Church*, ed. J. Bodensieck (Minneapolis: Augsburg Publishing House, 1965), 2452–2454. For more on the others, see Benjamin Kolodziej, "Early Lutheran Hymnody (1550–1650)," *Hymns and Hymnody*, vol. 2, 31–48.

The Only Son from Heaven

```
1 The    on - ly   Son from heav - en,   fore - told  by   an - cient  seers,
2 Oh,    time of   God ap - point - ed,  oh,   bright and ho - ly   morn!
3 A - wak - en,  Lord, our  spir - it    to   know and love  you    more,
4 O      Fa - ther, here be - fore  you  with  God  the  Ho - ly  Ghost,
```

```
      by  God   the  Fa - ther giv - en,  in   hu - man form ap - pears.
      He  comes, the  king  a - noint - ed,  the  Christ, the  vir - gin - born,
      in  faith  to  stand un - shak - en,  in  spir - it  to  a - dore,
      and  Je - sus, we   a - dore  you,  O  pride of  an - gel - host:
```

```
      No  sphere his  light con - fin - ing,  no  star  so  bright - ly
      grim death  to   van - quish for   us,  to  o - pen heav'n be -
      that  we, through this  world mov - ing,  each glimpse of  heav - en
      be - fore  you  mor - tals  low - ly,  cry,  "Ho - ly,  ho - ly,
```

```
      shin - ing   as   he,  our  Morn - ing   Star.
      fore  us    and  bring us  life  a - gain.
      prov - ing,  may  reap its  full - ness  there.
      ho - ly,  O   bless - ed  Trin - i - ty!"
```

Text: Elizabeth Cruciger, 1500–1535; tr. Arthur T. Russell, 1806–1874, alt.
Music: HERR CHRIST, DER EINIG GOTTS SOHN, *Enchiridion*, Erfurt, 1524

for various reasons including gender bias, to male authorship.[16] Even today her work is partly erased by insufficient translation and especially the omission of her concluding stanzas 4 and 5. In the modern hymnals mentioned above, the finale is a doxology taken from another source entirely.

---

16   See Mary Jane Haemig, "Elisabeth Cruciger (1500?–1535): The Case of the Disappearing Hymn Writer," *Sixteenth Century Journal* 32 (2001): 21–44. Timothy Wengert's translation of the full hymn, quoted here, is on p. 24, note 13. See also Joseph Herl's prose version in the *LSB Companion* 402, pp. 201–202. More recently, see Haemig's summary and Wengert's translation in Mary Jane Haemig, "Elisabeth Cruciger (ca. 1500–1535)," *Women Reformers of Early Modern Europe*, ed. Kirsi I. Stjerna (Minneapolis: Fortress Press, 2022), 34–42.

To appreciate Elisabeth Cruciger's biblical, historical, and theological expertise, we need to cite the full text. Her Latin schooling as a nun shows up right off in her allusion, "from the Father's heart," to Prudentius's *ex corde parentis* ("Of the Father's Love Begotten"). As in Luther's hymnody, the strategy is first to echo a known text and then to add the Reformation message. In her third stanza the language of love and sweetness echoes various medieval authors, as in the hymns attributed to Bernard of Clairvaux and multiple women/nuns called "mystics." "Let us, from your love drinking./ Of Wisdom take our fill./ Remain in faith, ne'er shrinking./ And serve the Spirit's will./ So our hearts, having tasted/ Your sweetness, never wasted,/ Will thirst alone for you." Especially in her final stanza, Elisabeth Cruciger's law and gospel dialectic shows her to be what Luther called a "theologian of the cross." "O slay us through your own goodness:/ Awaken us through grace./ Bring to the old such sickness,/ That we new life embrace./ Then we, on earth now dwelling,/ Your praises will be telling/ With mind and sense and tongue." Throughout, Cruciger's biblical artistry illustrates different facets of Christ as the "Morning Star" (Revelation 22:16), making it an Advent or Epiphany hymn sometimes placed adjacent to Philipp Nicolai's better-known "O Morning Star, How Fair and Bright," our next example of Lutheran hymnody. But first, there were some other examples of Reformation singing besides the Lutheran ones.

The Reformed and Other Traditions

Although Lutheran hymns spread quickly to the north in Swedish and English translations by Olaus Petri and Miles Coverdale, Switzerland, to the south, was another matter. Ulrich Zwingli (1484–1531) differed sharply with Luther on Christ and the Lord's Supper, culminating in their encounter at Marburg in 1529, and hymnody was another obvious difference. Zwingli's sharp break with Rome and his austere standards for worship meant no images and no hymns; indeed, he allowed no music at all, even for the Psalms, although he himself was a talented musician. So, there are no Zurich hymns to mention, at least not in the sixteenth-century Reformed context.

In Strasbourg, where the Psalter used Luther's translations, John Calvin (1509–64) picked up an idea that then flourished especially in Geneva: namely, fostering some congregational singing in French, although limited almost entirely to the Psalms. After all, he said, there could be no better texts to sing than the divine songs of Scripture. With the very limited exception of a biblical canticle like Simeon's *Nunc dimittis*, no other texts were sung in the Swiss or French Protestant realm. Like the Benedictines for centuries, but in French and with diverse melodies, Calvin's congregations sang the Psalter. Thus, the Reformed story of early hymn texts is brief.

Yet Calvin and his coworkers in this endeavor such as Clément Marot (ca. 1496–1544) and Theodore Beza (1519–1605) deserve mention and credit for their skillful poetic work on the Psalter. They stayed close to the original texts rather than paraphrasing Scripture loosely. Unlike Luther and later poets like Isaac Watts, they explicitly rejected the interpolation of Christian phrasing into Israel's Psalms. Their poetry employed different meters depending on the message of the Psalm and included rhymes in French to aid the memory.[17] Louis Bourgeois (ca. 1510–60), a talented musician in Geneva, provided many of the various melodies. By its completion in 1562, the Genevan or French Psalter provided all 150 texts for congregational singing, unaccompanied and in unison, with 125 different meters. Some of these melodies have endured in various contexts; what became known as OLD HUNDREDTH is surely the most familiar. Using this tune for Psalm 100 introduces the spread of Reformed Psalm singing to England, for in Geneva it was originally matched with Psalm 134. Later, however, it was used for the well-known English Psalm 100 hymn "All People That On Earth Do Dwell" (LBW 245, ELW 883, LSB 791), and has also become

---

17 For more, see Martin Tel, "Calvinist and Reformed Practices of Worship," *Historical Foundations of Worship*, ed. Melanie C. Ross and Mark A. Lamport (Grand Rapids, MI: Baker Academic, 2022), 178–191, especially 181–184.

common for doxologies and table prayers ever since (LBW 564–65, ELW 884–85, LSB 775, 805). The "Old Version" English Psalter of 1562 by Thomas Sternhold and John Hopkins, including some Lukan canticles and here represented by William Kethe's 1561 paraphrase of Psalm 100, has its own history, but again, one of music more than hymn texts. In that direction lies also the Scottish Psalter and the Bay Psalm Book of the "New World," first printed in 1640. Later, with Isaac Watts paraphrasing the Psalms in a free and explicitly Christian direction, the story of English hymn texts will resume. Meanwhile, back in sixteenth-century France, the Protestant or Huguenot singing of the Reformed Psalter extended not only to home use but also to public protests against the Roman Catholic government.[18]

Besides the Lutheran hymns and the Reformed Psalm-singing, there were only a few other examples of new sung texts in the Reformation era. As with Luther's first ballad hymn, the Anabaptists or Radical Reformers such as Menno Simons sang ballads for their many martyrs and a few other hymns. They are preserved in a hymnal from 1564/83 called *The Ausbund* and are still in use among the Amish.[19] Although the Council of Trent allowed new musical settings of certain texts, as seen in the compositions of Palestrina (1525–94), the Roman Catholic Church in the sixteenth century did not generate much new hymnody. Yet there is an interesting exception. "Lo, How a Rose E'er Blooming" (LBW 58, ELW 272, LSB 359) was apparently a pre-Reformation German Christmas carol, but it was first printed in a German Roman Catholic songbook in 1599—all twenty-three stanzas. As mentioned above, the rose was originally the Virgin Mary, but Protestants converted the reference to Christ. In abridged translations, it is still sung to the same melody and usually as arranged by the prolific composer Michael Praetorius (1571–1621), son of a Lutheran pastor.

---

18 Cornelius C. Simut, "John Calvin and the Complete French Psalter," *Hymns and Hymnody*, vol. 2, 52–54.

19 Westermeyer, *Te Deum*, 177.

8

LUTHERANS AND PIETISTS (1600–1750)

"Sing out! Ring out! . . . Tell the Story"

AFTER MARTIN LUTHER, western Christian history diversified dramatically, and so too, naturally, does the story of hymn texts. Soon there were not merely dozens of hymns, but hundreds of them, and many are still in use today. The "Protestants," as they were called early on, split into several different groups, and each had its own worship patterns and hymnody. Over time, these groups ended up sharing hymns across confessional lines, but that was a challenge. By the end of the sixteenth and especially into the seventeenth century, different confessions and thus diverging identities had hardened into opposing camps: Lutherans, Reformed (Presbyterians), the Anglican (Church of England) Episcopalians, various "Radical" or (Ana)Baptist groups, and a re-invigorated Roman Catholic "Counter-Reformation," too. The detailed theological polemics involved in these oppositions led to what many later called a period of "Orthodoxy" or Protestant Scholasticism, especially among the Lutherans and the Reformed in Germany and neighboring areas. This meant a heavy stress on strict and close distinctions between one's own truths and the errors of others.

At the same time, and in apparent contrast, this pattern overlaps with writings that exude a generous warmth of spiritual feelings or piety, indeed some of it under the later heading of "Pietism." Cold logic and warm sentiment are both found in texts of the era, as in a fifty-page preface defining "theology" with ever-narrowing distinctions, on the one hand, and a heartfelt endorsement of tender personal prayers, *Sacred Meditations,* on the other. Intriguingly, these two examples are from one and the same author, Johann Gerhard (1582–1637). So, this contrast should not stand for different movements or parties within Lutheranism; both types of writing can come from the same hand, whether Lutheran or Reformed or Roman Catholic. That "orthodox" and later "Pietist" sentiments could coexist in Lutheran authors and hymn writers should not surprise us, for Luther himself was credited with both careful theological distinctions (plus polemics) and also the fervent expressions of a relational piety, or "spirituality," to use twenty-first-century wording.

Indeed, the best-known hymns to come from early in this era, at the turn of the century around 1600, are from a versatile author of both types of literature, Philipp Nicolai. In an appendix to a long book, he added a pair of hymns: "Wake, Awake, for Night is Flying" and "O Morning Star, How Fair and Bright." They later became so standard in usage, with adaptations in J. S. Bach's cantatas and Felix Mendelssohn's oratorios, that they became known as the King and Queen of German chorales. Nicolai's texts lead us deep into his era, one of confessional controversies and spiritual longing, all in the context of a devastating plague. When his book and these hymns emphasize joy, it is in the teeth of staggering suffering and death.

Philipp Nicolai (1556–1608)

Philipp Nicolai

The son of a Lutheran pastor, Philipp Nicolai had an extensive theological education, culminating in Erfurt and Wittenberg, the very universities known for confessional distinctions and argumentation. Nicolai's writing career while a parish pastor continued this line of doctrinal polemics, not only against Rome but also and especially against the Reformed. In the 1580s and 1590s he wrote multiple large tomes against the "heretical sect" of the Calvinists, peaking in his 1599 *Mirror of the Evil Spirit that Moves in the Books of the Calvinists.* Yet in that same year he also wrote another "Mirror," his classic of spiritual comfort, *The Mirror of the Joy of Eternal Life,* including the two appended hymns that made him so well-known later. How his anti-Reformed polemics lived alongside these warm devotional hymns must await a look at the texts themselves.

For the moment, the context of his parish ministry in those years helps explain the concern for pastoral comfort: the plague. Nicolai's part of Germany was struck by a recurrence of the bubonic plague in the late 1590s, with an enormous death toll in his village and thus his parish. By one count, some 1,400 people died in his Westphalian town of 2,500. His ministerial records report 300 burials in July 1597 alone, with 170 deaths in one August week that year. The numbers are staggering and must have meant group funerals, which multiplied the grief and fear. His church and residence overlooked the cemetery and its endless mourning. Death seemed in charge, but Pastor Nicolai was steeped in a scriptural hope for new life, as expressed in his major work of spiritual consolation and expectation, the 1599 *Mirror of the Joy of Eternal Life.* Within the work, Nicolai quoted fully seven stanzas of Luther's "Dear Christians, One and All, Rejoice," but it is more important for his own pair of appended hymns.[1]

---

1   For a recent and full English translation of Nicolai's work, see Matthew Carver's rendering: Philipp Nicolai, *The Joy of Eternal Life* (St. Louis: Concordia Publishing House, 2021). The Luther hymn is quoted in chapter 8, 133–134 and 138–139. Of the four appended hymns, Carver supplies the traditional translations for these two and adds his own helpful, more literal prose translations of them, 271–276. Nicolai's

As noted earlier, the wedding imagery of bride and bridegroom has a long history in Christian literature, starting with the Bible and thus in hymn-writing. Yet, those who sing these two familiar hymns today may not immediately recognize the wedding theme, in part because of editorial decisions of translation and omission. Nicolai's tunes have a background too, with Luther himself and Hans Sachs the Meistersinger of major interest, but our focus is on the texts in both the original German and the English translations.[2]

"Wake, Awake, for Night Is Flying" (ELW 436, LSB 516)

Nicolai calls this the "Hymn of the Voice at Midnight and of the Wise Virgins, Who Go to Meet Their Heavenly Bridegroom (Matthew 25)." "Wake, Awake" was only three stanzas long, and thus has escaped later abridgements. The rendition in *Evangelical Lutheran Worship* (adapting Catherine Winkworth's translation) retains the initial letters of the three German stanzas (W, Z, G) by which Nicolai poetically honored his patron the Count (Graf) of Waldeck. Those who sang the hymn back then may or may not have noticed these capital letters, as with more recent patterns like FDR or JFK. *Wachet*/Wake, *Zion*, and *Gloria* also represent the fluid reception of German, Hebrew, and Latin words into English vocabulary. The "Morning Star" hymn gives a much fuller, indeed sevenfold, version of this naming of the Count, as presented below.

In general, staying alert or awake to greet the coming Savior may seem to be a natural theme for Advent, and indeed some hymnals have placed this hymn there. But the connection is not directly to Christmas, to the coming of Christ in the flesh. The

---

headers for these two hymns are here given in Carver's translation, 275 and 271 respectively.

2   For an essay on Nicolai's life and work, emphasizing his orthodox Lutheran doctrine, see Jonathan Mumme, "Philipp Nicolai (1556–1608): Mystic-Orthodox Polemicist," in *Lives and Writings of the Great Fathers of the Lutheran Church*, ed. T. Schmeling (St. Louis: Concordia Publishing House, 2016), 37–54. To be cited as *Lives and Writings*.

Wake, Awake, for Night Is Flying

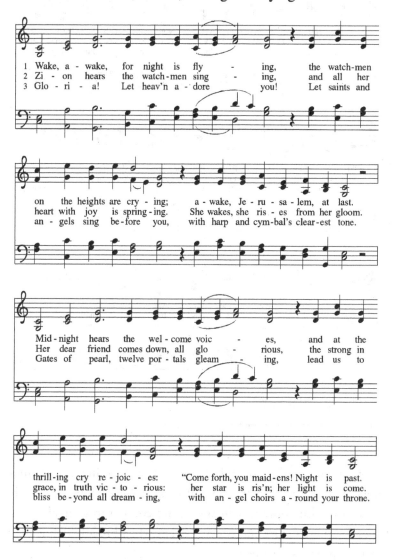

1 Wake, a - wake, for night is fly - ing, the watch-men
2 Zi - on hears the watch-men sing - ing, and all her
3 Glo - ri - a! Let heav'n a - dore you! Let saints and

on the heights are cry - ing; a - wake, Je - ru - sa - lem, at last.
heart with joy is spring-ing. She wakes, she ris - es from her gloom.
an - gels sing be-fore you, with harp and cym-bal's clear-est tone.

Mid - night hears the wel - come voic - es, and at the
Her dear friend comes down, all glo - rious, the strong in
Gates of pearl, twelve por - tals gleam - ing, lead us to

thrill-ing cry re - joic - es: "Come forth, you maid-ens! Night is past.
grace, in truth vic - to - rious: her star is ris'n; her light is come.
bliss be - yond all dream - ing, with an - gel choirs a - round your throne.

(Continued)

The bride - groom comes! A - wake; your lamps with glad - ness take!"
Now come, O Bless - ed One, Lord Je - sus, God's own Son.
No eye has caught the light, no ear the thun - d'ring might

Al - le - lu - ia! Rise and pre - pare the feast to share;
Sing ho - san - na! Oh, hear the call! Come one, come all,
of such glo - ry. There we will go: what joy we'll know!

go, meet the bride - groom, who draws near.
and fol - low to the ban - quet hall.
There sweet de - light will ev - er flow.

Text: Philipp Nicolai, 1556-1608; tr. composite
Music: WACHET AUF, Philipp Nicolai
Text © 1999 Augsburg Fortress.

deeper theme is the hopeful expectation of meeting Christ upon one's own death, as in the time of plague. Nevertheless, since the theme can also apply to Christ's second coming in general as part of eschatology or the end times, Advent when broadly defined can be an appropriate context.

In the first stanza, the call to awake is quickly applied to "maidens" with lamps who are awaiting a wedding feast, as in Nicolai's header naming Jesus's parable in Matthew 25. The story is familiar: some bridesmaids, but not all, were ready with their lamps. "The bridegroom comes!

Awake. Your lamps with gladness take!" Stanza two expands this wedding theme to specify the bride as Zion or Israel, God's beloved, as in Isaiah 62 or Jeremiah or the entire Song of Songs as traditionally understood. In the New Testament, the bride is identified with the church and Christ is the bridegroom, as in 2 Corinthians 11, Ephesians 5, and Revelation 21. As noted regarding Bernard of Clairvaux and Luther, the wedding theme was for centuries a normal and biblical way to speak of the soul's relationship to Christ. Victorian translators toned down the bodily and sexual aspects of this language, and in some cases, such as Nicolai's "Morning Star," eliminated it completely, but "Wake, Awake" retains the general idea. "Her star is risen" points to the Morning Star as Christ, as in the companion hymn. In Nicolai's original, the wedding feast is not just a "banquet hall" as in the ELW version at the end of stanza 2, but the *Abendmahl*; literally, the "evening meal" but also the normal name for the Lord's Supper, a major topic for Nicolai overall. Thus, in one version (LSB 516, st. 2) it is "To eat the Supper at Thy call."

Stanza three adds our singing of "Gloria" to the watchmen's song and the angel chorus at the gates of pearl, all in joyful expectation of meeting Christ in glory beyond sight and sound. The original finale goes beyond normal German words, with "io io!" and using Latin for the "sweet delight" (*in dulci jubilo*) of the heavenly encounter. Thus could Nicolai's beleaguered congregation sing now about the singing to come, and be comforted.

J. S. Bach's beloved cantata 140 (*Wachet auf, ruft uns die Stimme*) took Nicolai's text further. All three stanzas are sung in their entirety by the choir, with variations of harmony and a striking lyrical (counter-) melody for stanza two, later adapted for an organ chorale (Schübler Chorale, BWV 645). It was composed in 1731 for the very Sunday (27th after Trinity) when Jesus's parable of the maidens and their lamps was the Gospel reading. Between the hymn texts comes some additional poetry, apparently anonymous, expressing the wedding theme in the evocative longing of the soprano bride and the bass Christ. In rhythmic alternation and close harmony they unite their voices and desires: "My beloved is mine! And I am his! [United] Where pleasure in fullness, where joy will abound."[3] In Bach's compositional hands, these texts seem to anticipate the operatic intercourse, so to speak, of Mozart or Verdi, but the cantata is better understood as growing out of the biblical imagery and tradition that was famous in Bernard of Clairvaux and embedded in Nicolai's text.

Before moving on to Nicolai's other hymn, where the bridal theme has not fared as well in modern translations, we should note that the union of the believer and Christ in "Wake, Awake" has a sacramental dimension that may partially explain the author's antipathy to the Calvinists. With *Abendmahl* clearly named, and a bodily uniting suggested, it should be no surprise that Nicolai was firmly committed to the traditional Lutheran teaching of the "real presence" of Christ in the Lord's Supper, and thus a communicant's union with the full Christ in the receiving of his body and blood. So, too, the "Morning Star" hymn has a central place for Christ's body and blood, indeed in the central line of the central (fourth) stanza, even if it is obscured in many hymnal translations/omissions. In Nicolai's view, the Calvinists denied this truth, forfeiting union with Christ and thus forfeiting Christian fellowship. Perhaps his ferocious attacks on the Calvinists and his hymn of gentle comfort are not so antithetical as they may seem.

"O Morning Star, How Fair and Bright!"
(ELW 308, LSB 395)

Nicolai presented his other 1599 hymn under the heading "A Spiritual Wedding Hymn of the Believing Soul concerning Jesus Christ, its Heavenly Bridegroom, based on the 45th Psalm." Yet in modern hymnals the Morning Star has often been stripped of the theme of a bride and her bridegroom. The first letters of these seven stanzas also point to Nicolai's territorial ruler at the time: Wilhelm Ernst, Count (Graf) and Lord for Waldeck (WEGVHZW). As with the briefer acrostic in

---

3   For a deeper analysis of these texts, see Michael Marissen and Daniel R. Melamed, https://bachcantatatexts.org/BWV140.htm, accessed August 22, 2022.

O Morning Star, How Fair and Bright!

1 O Morn - ing Star, how fair and bright! You shine with
2 Come, pre - cious dia - mond, light di - vine, and deep with -
3 Lord, when you look on us in love, at once there
4 Al - might - y Fa - ther, in your Son you loved us,

God's own truth and light, a - glow with grace and mer - cy!
in our hearts now shine; there light a flame un - dy - ing!
falls from God a - bove a ray of pur - est plea - sure.
when not yet be - gun was this old earth's foun - da - tion!

Of Ja - cob's line, King Da - vid's son, our Lord and Sav - ior,
In your one bod - y let us be as liv - ing branch - es
Your word and Spir - it, flesh and blood re - fresh our souls with
Your Son has ran - somed us in love to live in him here

you have won our hearts to serve you on - ly! Low - ly,
of a tree, your life our lives sup - ply - ing. Now, though
heav'n-ly food. You are our dear - est trea - sure! Let your
and a - bove: this is your great sal - va - tion. Al - le -

ho - ly! Great and glo - rious, all vic - to - rious, rich
dai - ly earth's deep sad - ness may per - plex us and
mer - cy warm and cheer us! Oh, draw near us! For
lu - ia! Christ the liv - ing, to us giv - ing life

in bless - ing! Rule and might o'er all pos - sess - ing!
dis - tress us, yet with heav'n - ly joy you bless us.
you teach us God's own love through you has reached us.
for - ev - er, keeps us yours and fails us nev - er!

(Continued)

5 Oh, let the harps break forth in sound!
  Our joy be all with music crowned,
  our voices gaily blending!
  For Christ goes with us all the way—
  today, tomorrow, ev'ry day!
  His love is never ending!
  Sing out! Ring out!
  Jubilation!
  Exultation!
  Tell the story!
  Praise to Christ, who reigns in glory!

6 What joy to know, when life is past,
  the Lord we love is first and last,
  the end and the beginning!
  He will one day, oh, glorious grace,
  transport us to that happy place
  beyond all tears and sinning!
  Amen! Amen!
  Come, Lord Jesus!
  Crown of gladness!
  We are yearning
  for the day of your returning.

Text: Philipp Nicolai, 1556–1608; tr. *Lutheran Book of Worship*
Music: WIE SCHÖN LEUCHTET, Philipp Nicolai
Text © 1978 *Lutheran Book of Worship*, admin. Augsburg Fortress.

"Wake, Awake," this poetic tribute carried a personal and poignant message, since the young Count, once Nicolai's pupil, had died of the plague in 1598.

Although the star in the title has often led to an Epiphany placement in modern hymnals, the "bright morning star" is not the star of Bethlehem but Christ himself (Revelation 22:16, with Numbers 24:17) as also in "Wake, Awake." Scriptural references abound in this text; by one count there are thirty phrases from fifteen different biblical books, with Revelation and Psalm 45 about a bridal couple especially prominent. Right off, modern versions drop the naming of Christ as the bridegroom. "You, David's son of Jacob's line, my king and bridegroom" became "Of Jacob's line, King David's son, our Lord and Savior" (in ELW 308, st. 1, see also LSB 395). Similarly, the original second stanza has a warmer personal tone in its references to eating spiritual food than most modern translations: "my heart names you a heavenly flower; your sweet gospel is pure milk and honey. O my little blossom, hosanna! Your heavenly manna that we eat I can never forget." Nicolai's next two stanzas have been compressed into one, and evocative lines dropped, such as "Take me lovingly in your arms." The next one (ELW 308, st. 4) again deletes the bridal language: "Your son has betrothed me to himself; he is my treasure, I his bride." To round out the list of omissions, Nicolai's penultimate stanza personalizes the longing for the beloved: "that I might dwell with Jesus dear, my wonderful handsome bridegroom, in constant love."

In general, the entire original text is in this singular voice of a bride, as in Nicolai's own title, "A Spiritual Wedding Hymn of the Believing Soul." But modern translators have transposed it into a general plural ("we") and have deleted most of the marital theme. Victorian prudery may have influenced earlier English versions, and some recent editorial opposition to binary, heterosexual, gendered language seems to support that change. Nevertheless, the German text as sung through the generations has retained the theme.[4]

"Morning Star" closes with Nicolai's familiar theme of joy and hope over against the plague's relentless march of disease, funerals, and burials. "Sing out! Ring out! Jubilation! Exultation! Tell the Story!" (st. 5). "He will one day, oh, glorious grace, transport us to that happy place beyond all tears and sinning!" (st. 6).

J. S. Bach used this hymn often, especially for cantata 1 but also for parts of other cantatas, and Felix Mendelssohn used Nicolai's hymns for his oratorios. Such classical usage reflected and contributed to its central place in the early modern canon of hymns. In the nineteenth century, *Wachet auf* and *Morgenstern* were crowned by Christian D. F. Palmer (1811–75) as the King and Queen of chorales, itself also a marital allusion. Philipp Nicolai's place in the standard repertory of hymnody was secure and introduces us to the fervent spiritual longing that characterized what later became associated with Pietism. The German Pietists, including the Moravians, influenced a whole range of other confessions and language groups, especially some Swedes and the Wesleyans in England. How that started requires a segue of continents and centuries.

From Germans and Pietists to Swedes and Wesleyans

The spiritual side of Philipp Nicolai and Johann Gerhard mentioned earlier also found expression in the many writings of Johann Arndt (1555–1621),

---

4   Routley-Richardson, *Panorama* #188–89, provides the German texts for both hymns and multiple translations.

such as *True Christianity* around 1610. There was a broad spiritual movement among some German Lutherans in the mid-seventeenth century, and it involved great hymnody. Paul Gerhardt has already been introduced for his adaptation of a medieval tradition for Good Friday, "O Sacred Head, Now Wounded" (ELW 351–52 and LSB 449–50). Living through plague and war, this poet-theologian was a pastor near and in Berlin where he worked with composer-cantor Johann Crüger (1598–1662).[5] Besides the immortal "Sacred Head," modern hymnals also feature Gerhardt's contributions to Advent, Christmas, Lent, and Easter,[6] as well as "Evening and Morning" (ELW 761 and LSB 726) and his beloved "Now Rest beneath Night's Shadow" (ELW 568 and LSB 880). John Wesley himself translated Gerhardt's "Jesus, Thy Boundless Love to Me" (LSB 683). His texts live on not only in his hymns—over a hundred of them, with many sung today in dozens of languages—but also in multiple cantatas by J. S. Bach and G. P. Telemann.

In general, this era produced so many hymns that only a few names can be mentioned here; the *Lutheran Service Book* has fully seventy hymns dating from 1622 to 1674.[7] Martin Rinckhart (1586–1649) wrote dozens of hymns, notably "Now Thank We All Our God" (ELW 839–40 and LSB 895), while also living through war, famine, and a horrific 1637 plague. Johann Heermann (1585–1647) authored the classic "Ah, Holy Jesus" (ELW 349 and LSB 439 using

---

5   For more on Gerhardt, see Gerald Krispin, "Paul Gerhardt (1607–76)," in *Lives and Writings*, 229–242.

6   For Advent, "O Lord, How Shall I Meet You" (ELW 241 and LSB 334); for Christmas, "All My Heart Again Rejoices" (ELW 273 and LSB 360) and "O Jesus Christ, Thy Manger Is" (LSB 372); for Lent, "A Lamb Goes Uncomplaining Forth" (ELW 340 and LSB 438, see also LSB 453); for Easter, "Awake My Heart, with Gladness" (ELW 378 and LSB 467). Gerhardt is represented still further in the LSB: 596, 724, 737, 754, 756, 788. For a recent overview of Gerhardt, see Hans Schwarz, "Trust in God in Trying Times: The Hymns of Paul Gerhardt," *Word and World* 43.2 (Spring 2023): 175–183.

7   See Joseph Herl's essay "Germany from 1620 to the Present" in the *LSB Companion*, vol. 2, 27–50, with the list on 31–33.

the Winkworth translation for fifteen stanzas) as well as others (ELW 675 and LSB 839, ELW 806 and LSB 696). For one more example, countless Lutheran congregations have sung the communion hymn by Johann Franck (1618–77), "Soul, Adorn Yourself with Gladness," which is also saturated with marital imagery (ELW 488 and LSB 636) as well as his "Jesus, Priceless Treasure" (ELW 775 and LSB 743). These seventeenth-century German hymns, marked by Lutheran ortho-doxy and spiritual piety, gradually became common in hymnals of all denominations.[8]

When Philipp Jakob Spener (1635–1705) wrote a preface to a new edition of Johann Arndt's sermons in 1675 and then published it as a booklet, the title of *Pia Desideria,* or Heartfelt Wishes, provided a name for an emerging movement. "Pietism" became associated with lay groups meeting independently for prayer and scripture study, some of them beyond Lutheran confessional boundaries. August Herman Francke (1663–1727), from his position as Pastor and a Professor at the University of Halle, channeled these devotional energies around 1700 into societal agencies such as an orphanage, schools for children, a hospital, and then a training center for missionaries, all of which became known as the Francke Foundations. From this point, German Pietism with its hymnody spread to so many confessions and countries in Europe, the New World, and mission fields that no single sketch can cover it all. The hymns of German Pietists will connect several chapters of this story going forward. From Germany, such hymns spread to Scandinavia, to England with its colonies, and to mission fields around the world. Nordic Lutherans brought them to the United States, and English Methodists sang them at Wesleyan revival meetings on both sides of the Atlantic. German Pietist hymnody also grounded Walter Rauschenbusch, American theologian of the Social Gospel, almost two centuries later. To follow these connections, we need to go beyond Lutheran orthodoxy, specifically, to include the Moravians.

---

8   For texts by Gerhardt, Rinckhart, Heermann, and Franck, in German and En-glish, see Routley-Richardson, *Panorama* #191–96, pp. 188–201.

Shaped at the Francke Foundations and the University of Halle, Nicolaus von Zinzendorf (1700–60) named his large estate in Saxony "Herrnhut" and welcomed some Protestant refugees from Roman Catholic Bohemia who became known as the Moravian Brethren. Zinzendorf himself wrote hundreds of hymns, some of them with long legacies such as "Jesus, Still Lead On" (ELW 624, LSB 718). Another, "Jesus, Your Blood and Righteousness" (LBW 302, LSB 563, translated by John Wesley), hints at a theme that he took to some excess according to his critics, namely, the blood and wounds of Christ, and especially his side wound. Apart from controversies over their original Lutheran patron, the Moravian Brethren spread through Germany to neighboring countries, like Denmark, and more specifically for our story to Sweden and to England.

Skipping to the nineteenth century, hymnals of the Swedish Moravians influenced Carl Olof Rosenius (1816–68) and thus a Pietist revival movement in Sweden. Lina Sandell (1832–1903), daughter of a "Rosenian" Pietist pastor, wrote poetry and hymns from an early

† LINA BERG,
den kända författarinnan under
signaturen "L. S.", afled i Stockholm den 27 juli.

Lina Sandell

age and later worked as an editor alongside Rosenius himself. Upon her confirmation and first communion, she wrote to her sister of her "wedding day" and her "heavenly bridegroom": "He is mine and I am his." Her early hymn "Children of the Heavenly Father" (ELW 781, LSB 725) gives tender expression to a parent-child sort of piety and became a beloved baptismal hymn in Sweden. Later married and thus also known as Carolina (Lina) Sandell Berg, she wrote hundreds of hymns. Those still in wide use include "Day by Day" (ELW 790) and "Thy Holy Wings" (ELW 613, see also ELW 683), expanding on Jesus's comparison of himself to a mother hen (Matthew 23:37) and perhaps following Zinzendorf's own earlier interest in that image to emphasize God's mothering aspect.[9] Alongside other Nordic Pietist hymns, Sandell's many songs became immensely popular also in neighboring Norway and in the Scandinavian-American immigrant communities of the United States. That she became known as "Sweden's Fanny Crosby" will make more sense when we get to that other prolific hymn-writing woman in the United States whose texts have also been sung across many languages and denominations.

The Moravians also had a direct and earlier impact on the English-speaking world, from eighteenth-century Britain to its colonies. Groups appeared in London, for example, and one particular 1735 voyage to the New World can stand for our passage to a new section in this saga. When Atlantic storms roiled their ship, the Moravians prayed and sang some of their German Pietist hymns. Their calm confidence and its musical expression so impressed their fellow seafarers that two brothers on board took note and later gave credit. Ever after, John and Charles Wesley took a special interest in such hymns

---

9   For Sandell, including the quotations, see Gracia Grindal, *Preaching from Home: The Stories of Seven Lutheran Women Hymn Writers* (Grand Rapids, MI: Eerdmans, 2011), 169 and 196–198, plus 200–214 for her legacy in the United States. See also the imagery of Jesus's wings in Paul Gerhardt's "Now Rest" (ELW 568 and LSB 880), with commentary in the *ELW Companion* on ELW 613.

as expressions of a fervent faith. John Wesley translated some of them and commended the Moravian model to his poet brother Charles who wrote his own, too many to count. So, the Wesleys now enter the picture, along with the whole history of the Methodists, thus influenced by German Pietist hymnody.

✦ **9** ✦

ISAAC WATTS AND THE WESLEY BROTHERS (1700-1800)

"Oh, for a Thousand Tongues to Sing"

Isaac Watts (1674–1748)

ISAAC WATTS STARTS off our encounter with English hymnody, although he himself credited others as the real pioneers. In his youth, only the official Anglican Church of England was allowed, so "nonconformists" such as his own father worshipped illegally and sometimes went to jail for it. With the "Declaration of Indulgence" in 1688, the king eased the pressure on Congregational and Independent churches like the one Watts served, Mark Lane Chapel in London. A more Calvinist type of nonconformist Protestantism, stemming from the Reformed

Isaac Watts

tradition in France/Switzerland and the Low Countries, insisted that only scriptural praise should be sung, most typically the Psalms. The "metrical psalter," already introduced with its translations and difficult melodies, prevailed for a time in many parts of England, and for a long time among the Scottish Presbyterians and some American Puritans.

Watts, however, citing the precedent of the 1694 Psalm paraphrases of John Patrick (1632–95), composed free versions of the Psalms and some entirely new hymn texts. His 1707 *Hymns and Spiritual Songs* contained such Psalm paraphrases, freer songs, and communion hymns. Some of these have lived on for centuries, such as ELW 782 "My Shepherd, You Supply My Need" (Psalm 23). In 1719, Watts went further with loose paraphrases of the Psalms in a Christian direction, as indicated in the work's title: *The Psalms of David Imitated in the Language of the New Testament*. It was immediately quite popular, in church and at home. Many Watts hymns sung today are in fact paraphrases of verses from the Psalms: "O That the Lord Would Guide My Ways" (part of Psalm 119 in ELW 772 and LSB 707), "Give to Our God Immortal Praise" (Psalm 136 in ELW 848), and even the explicitly Christian "Jesus Shall Reign" (part of Psalm 72 in ELW 434 and LSB 832). A Watts paraphrase could be quite free indeed, substituting England for Israel, as an example. Under his creative pen, the second half of Psalm 98 makes it sound like the coming Lord is Christ himself in "Joy to the World" (ELW 267 and LSB 387), even without any explicitly Christian phrasing. Furthermore, Watts's new hymns served not only to praise God but also to teach the gospel to the congregation, often in tandem with the sermon. "When I Survey the Wondrous Cross" (ELW 803 and LSB 425) fits this role, as does "Alas! And Did My Savior Bleed" (ELW 337 and LSB 437), cherished by later American evangelicals such as Fanny Crosby for prompting her conversion.[1]

---

1   For further hymns by Watts, see ELW 847, LSB 705 and 812, any Methodist hymnal, or *Congregational Praise* (1951) with forty-five of them. For more on Watts

O God, Our Help in Ages Past

1 O God, our help in a - ges past, our hope for years to come,
2 Un - der the shad - ow of your throne your saints have dwelt se - cure;
3 Be - fore the hills in or - der stood or earth re - ceived its frame,
4 A thou-sand a - ges in your sight are like an eve - ning gone,

our shel - ter from the storm-y blast, and our e - ter - nal home:
suf - fi - cient is your arm a - lone, and our de - fense is sure.
from ev - er - last - ing you are God, to end - less years the same.
short as the watch that ends the night be - fore the ris - ing sun.

5 Time, like an ever-rolling stream,
bears all our years away;
they fly forgotten, as a dream
dies at the op'ning day.

6 O God, our help in ages past,
our hope for years to come,
still be our guard while troubles last
and our eternal home.

Text: Isaac Watts, 1674–1748, alt.
Music: ST. ANNE, William Croft, 1678–1727

As restrictions on the non-conformists seemed to loom again around 1714, Watts rendered the opening of Psalm 90 as his enduring "Our God, Our Help in Ages Past" (ELW 632 and LSB 733), originally in nine stanzas. His close yet poetic treatment of Psalm 90:4–5 (st. 4: "A thousand ages in your sight . . .") also illustrates what can happen when older poetry meets current usage. Amid the correct concern of the 1970s to convert gendered wording to inclusive language, the *Lutheran Book of Worship* (320) changed Watt's original fifth stanza ("Time like an ever-rolling stream bears all its sons away; They fly forgotten, as a dream . . .") into "Time . . . soon bears us all away; We fly forgotten, as a dream . . ." The LBW editors did not recognize the "sons of time" as a poetic expression for the years, even with the explicit warrant in Psalm 90:4, leaving the neutered text to contradict

himself, see Rochelle A. Stackhouse, "Isaac Watts, Composer of Psalms and Hymns," in *Hymns and Hymnody*, vol. 2, 197–209 and the other literature cited there.

the scriptural witness (Isaiah 49) that God does not forget us. The ELW 632 version restores the intent ("Time . . . bears all our years away; they fly forgotten"), yet *Lutheran Worship* (1982) 180 and LSB 733 have continued the politically correct but faulty editing.

When John Wesley edited and published this hymn, he tweaked the start ("Our God") to become "O God, Our Help . . .", as in many current hymnals, and reduced the original nine stanzas, thus illustrating how the Wesleys adopted and lightly adapted Watts's legacy. Further, their early associate George Whitefield used Watts's hymns extensively, including in American revival meetings as also shared in some African American hymnals. In that vein, revivalist musician Robert Lowry in 1868 added a chorus to Watts to yield "Come, We That Love the Lord; We're Marching to Zion" (ELW 625 and LSB 669). "I Love the Lord, He Heard My Cry," the Watts paraphrase of Psalm 116, later became beloved via some African American hymnals (*African American Heritage Hymnal* 395), although such metered call and response singing did not require hymnals at all. In general, the Watts hymns still have an impressive ecumenical reach today.

The Wesley Brothers

John Wesley (1703–91) and Charles Wesley (1707–88) are rightly famous for several reasons: leadership of the new "Methodist" movement first within the Church of England (Anglican) and then on the American scene, powerful sermons and theological tracts, and of course a prolific output of hymnody now sung in churches of all kinds. Their major theme was holiness, and when we sing Charles Wesley's "Love Divine, All Loves Excelling" we are in the middle of Methodist disputes over sanctification. And there are so many Wesleyan warhorses in our hymnals. "Hark, the Herald Angels Sing" (ELW 270 and LSB 380) is a cultural commonplace, and "Oh, for a Thousand Tongues to Sing" (ELW 886 and LSB 528) is among the best-known hymns in

Protestant circles especially. That both of these familiar titles refer to singing (plus "sings music in the sinner's ears") is no accident, for the Wesleyan movement was fueled by song, by hundreds even thousands of them. In the overall history of hymnody, the work of the Wesleys was a bridge between the German, especially Moravian, Pietist tradition and an American "Holiness" movement. The eventful sea voyage to the New World mentioned earlier can represent this crossing.

Sons of an Anglican (Church of England) priest, John and Charles Wesley were well educated in their musical home and at Oxford University, but no one could have predicted the prolific output of sermons and treatises by John or the poems and hymns by Charles, much less their global impact on church history. Their learning and piety were early on dedicated to evangelism, including missions to the American colonies. So, in late 1735 the young men found themselves on board The Simmonds *en route* to Georgia with Moravian missionaries as shipmates and amid a terrifying storm. Calmly singing German hymns from their new Song Book (*Das Gesang-Buch*), the Moravians inspired the Wesley brothers to deepen their appreciation for hymnody, especially these hymns, namely, to translate some of these Pietist texts, to write their own, and to collect them in hymnals.

Their trip to the American colonies was brief, but the connection bore fruit over time. The Wesleys were very open about the inspiration they received from the Lutheran and Pietist tradition, especially by way of the Moravian Peter Böhler upon their return to England. John famously reported that his heart was "strangely warmed" on hearing a reading of Martin Luther's exposition of St. Paul's proclamation of grace. Charles directly cited Böhler in the hymn he wrote to mark the first anniversary of his own conversion. Originally eighteen verses but quickly reduced, "Oh, for a Thousand Tongues to Sing" (ELW 886 and LSB 528) opens by quoting Böhler's own eagerness to proclaim. Thus, the German Pietist movement and hymnody found fertile soil in the Wesleyans, even when they broke from the Moravians, and such hymns then flourished in both England and the United States.

John Wesley (1703–91) as Translator and Editor

John Wesley

John Wesley's long career in translating as well as collecting, editing, and publishing hymns began immediately upon his arrival in Georgia. In 1737 he published *Psalms and Hymns* in Charleston, South Carolina, with half of the hymns by Isaac Watts and a few by George Herbert (*The Temple*), but also five of his translations from *Das Gesang-Buch* published by Zinzendorf, including hymns by Johann Freylinghausen and Zinzendorf himself. This book, now exceedingly rare, was not only the first of many Wesleyan hymnals but also the first true hymnal in America (or England!), setting the Psalters aside. Thus, as translator and as hymnal editor, J. Wesley deserves our attention, even if his younger brother's hymns became more famous.

Starting with that shipboard encounter, John Wesley went on to translate thirty-three German hymns from Zinzendorf's 1735 Song Book.[2] A scholar and linguist, he also translated from French and Spanish sources, but his presence in hymnals today stems from the German hymnody. From that Moravian Song Book, Wesley translated hymns by Freylinghausen, Gerhard Tersteegen, and Johann Scheffler ("Thee Will I Serve," SBH 505 and LBW 502; see LSB 694 for the Winkworth translation), as well as four by Paul Gerhardt and eight by Zinzendorf himself. Gerhardt's "Jesus, Thy Boundless Love to Me" had sixteen stanzas in the Wesley brothers' 1739 *Hymns and Sacred Poems*, then nine in the influential 1780 *Collection of Hymns* that became the main Methodist hymnal. Even reduced these days to four stanzas (SBH 399 uses stanzas 1–4, LBW 336 and LSB 683 use stanzas 1, 2, 4, and 16), Wesley's eloquent expression of Gerhardt's fervent faith comes through clearly. The 1739 collection presents the text with its own header but otherwise almost exactly as in modern hymnals, as evident here in stanza 1:

Living by CHRIST.

From the German.

JESU, *thy boundless Love to me*
No Thought can reach, no Tongue declare:
O knit my thankful Heart to Thee,
And reign without a Rival there.
Thine wholly, thine alone I am:
Be Thou alone my constant Flame.[3]

---

2   John Nuelsen, *John Wesley and the German Hymn* (Calverley: A. S. Holbrook, 1972), appends all thirty-three hymns, every stanza, in the German original and in Wesley's translation. Details in this section are from Nuelsen's book, a translation from the original German.

3   *Hymns and Sacred Poems*, edited by John Wesley and Charles Wesley (London: Wm Strahan, 1739); facsimile edition (Madison, NJ: The Charles Wesley Society, 2007), 156.

In Zinzendorf's own classic "Jesus, Thy Blood and Righteousness," the reduction of stanzas is even more dramatic. Originally in thirty-three stanzas, Wesley's version retained twenty-four in the 1740 edition of *Hymns and Sacred Poems,* but only ten by the time of the 1780 *Collection of Hymns,* and just six in recent Lutheran hymnals (LBW 302 and LSB 563). Nevertheless, Wesley's gifts as a translator show their enduring value here, as well.

Besides these translations, John Wesley, sometimes aided by his brother Charles, collected, edited, and occasionally introduced hundreds of hymns in dozens of hymnals, with revisions and reprints too numerous even to list. His Preface to *Select Hymns* (1761) also includes some forceful "Directions" on *how* to sing: in unison, in time, and not too loudly ("don't bawl") or too softly. Two of the hymnals mentioned already, the early and pioneering *Psalms and Hymns* (1737) and the later and enduring *Collection of Hymns for the People Called Methodist* (1780) are not only rough chronological bookends but also key examples of two different types of Wesleyan hymnals.[4] The latter *Collection of Hymns* was the culmination of a long series of hymnals specifically for Methodist gatherings outside of the official Church of England Sunday services, whether in homes or outdoors. This series began with the first edition of *Hymns and Sacred Poems* (1739), a title also suggesting personal use. There were further editions in 1740, 1743, and 1756. Although the original Wesleyan movement attempted to coexist as a reforming impulse within the established Church of England, especially regarding Sunday communion services, such hymnal titles as *Hymns and Spiritual Songs, Intended for the Use of Real Christians of all Denominations* (1752) hint at the growing tensions that in fact did lead to a new denomination. The other type of hymnal, stemming from the colonial *Psalms and Hymns* in 1737 with its eleven editions in that century, was for

---

4   Robin A. Leaver, "*Psalms and Hymns* and *Hymns and Sacred Poems:* Two Strands of Wesleyan Hymn Collections," *Music and the Wesleys,* edited by Nicholas Temperley and Stephen Banfield (Chicago: University of Illinois, 2010), 41–51.

Sunday morning worship, as fully evident by 1784. In that very year when John Wesley at eighty years old finally violated Episcopal polity by ordaining clergy on his own, he published *Psalms and Hymns for the Lord's Day*, and the break of Methodists from Anglicans became a denominational reality. Charles Wesley, however, was loyal to the Church of England throughout his life, and it is to his poetic pen that posterity owes the famous Wesleyan hymns.

Charles Wesley (1707–88) as Hymn Writer

Charles Wesley

By all accounts, Charles Wesley wrote poetry almost every day, from childhood to death bed, with his daily journals becoming a multi-volume anthology of these poetic reflections. Such verses, only some-times meant to be sung, were usually musings on church affairs, or the biblical text of the day or season, or family life such as a son's bad toothache. The incredible total of 9,000 poems from his pen yielding 6,000 hymns becomes imaginable, although still amazing, when we picture him writing such a poem every other day for fifty years.[5] As they say, do the math: 180 a year for 50 years is 9,000.

The "Methodist" phenomenon inspired by the Wesley brothers has often been considered *Theology in Hymns*, to cite a pertinent book title.[6] Indeed, the movement's emphases, and thus the related theological controversies, show up in many of Charles Wesley's hymn texts, whether expressing Pietist sentiments or opposing Calvinist doctrines. Within the movement itself a dispute arose over sanctification or perfection. How much holiness or freedom from sin should the convert hope for in this life? Was such progress sudden or gradual? Textual details in one particular hymn reflect this dispute.

"Love Divine, All Loves Excelling" (ELW 631, LSB 700)

As in his poetry generally, with "Love Divine, All Loves Excelling" Charles Wesley in 1747 invoked and reapplied a classic line, in this case not from Scripture but from an English poem by one of the island's greats, John Dryden in his 1691 opera "King Arthur": "Fairest Isle, all Isles Excelling." The hymn was originally sung to the very tune Henry Purcell supplied for Dryden's song, now used more often for "Christ is Made the Sure Foundation." Thus, in the opening line and the tune as well, the original singers of "Love Divine" could be well aware that Wesley was intentionally pitting divine love against human love, for Dryden's second line about their fair island was "Seat of pleasures and of love."

Although brief, the hymn text has nevertheless often suffered the omission of the second of its four stanzas (even in John Wesley's 1780 hymnal), and some textual tweaks, all because of a dispute over sanctification. Originally, Charles wrote "Let us all in thee inherit; let us find thy second rest. Take away our power of sinning" (st. 2). The nuances of difference about sanctification among the early Wesleyans,

---

5   For more on Charles Wesley and his many hymns, see John R. Tyson, *Assist Me to Proclaim: The Life and Hymns of Charles Wesley* (Grand Rapids, MI: Eerdmans, 2007).

6   Teresa Berger, *Theology in Hymns* (Nashville: Abingdon, 1985).

Love Divine, All Loves Excelling

1 Love di - vine, all loves ex - cel - ling, Joy of heav'n, to
2 Breathe, oh, breathe thy lov - ing Spir - it in - to ev - 'ry
3 Come, Al - might - y, to de - liv - er; let us all thy
4 Fin - ish then thy new cre - a - tion, pure and spot - less

earth come down! Fix in us thy hum - ble dwell-ing, all thy
trou - bled breast; let us all in thee in - her - it; let us
life re - ceive; sud - den - ly re - turn, and nev - er, nev - er -
let us be; let us see thy great sal - va - tion per - fect -

faith - ful mer - cies crown. Je - sus, thou art all com - pas - sion,
find thy prom - ised rest. Take a - way the love of sin - ning;
more thy tem - ples leave. Thee we would be al - ways bless - ing,
ly re - stored in thee! Changed from glo - ry in - to glo - ry,

pure, un - bound - ed love thou art; vis - it us with
Al - pha and O - me - ga be; end of faith, as
serve thee as thy hosts a - bove, pray, and praise thee
till in heav'n we take our place, till we cast our

(Continued)

thy   sal - va - tion,   en - ter   ev - 'ry   trem - bling heart.
its   be - gin - ning,   set   our   hearts   at   lib - er - ty.
with - out   ceas - ing,   glo - ry   in   thy   per - fect   love.
crowns   be - fore   thee,   lost   in   won - der, love,   and   praise!

Text: Charles Wesley, 1707–1788
Music: HYFRYDOL, Rowland H. Prichard, 1811–1887

even between the brothers, need not detain us long, but the original expression "second rest" (second blessing), meaning a surge of earthly sanctification, has often been changed to "promised rest" (as in ELW 631 and LSB 700). "Take away our power of sinning" was doubly problematic, not only for the lofty ideal that such could be possible in this life but also for the implied loss of free will to sin, or to refrain from sinning. It early on seemed safer to say, "Take away *the love* of sinning." The last stanza could also cause concern over an inflated expectation for earthly holiness ("pure and sinless/spotless let us be") but the conclusion as a whole points with Revelation 4 and 7 toward a final or heavenly goal ("'til in heaven we take our place") where such perfection or complete sanctification is anticipated. Ever the poet, here too Charles borrowed a spiritual, even mystical, phrase of eschatological hope. "Lost in wonder, love and praise" comes from Joseph Addison (LBW 264). In general, framing spiritual progress or sanctification in terms of its fulfillment or perfection in heaven avoids the criticism of expecting too much holiness on earth.

Charles Wesley was loyal to the Church of England to the end, even to his choice of burial ground. His brother John's eventual support for ordination outside of the Anglican succession, especially for the mission field, charted a more independent or Methodist course for the spread of the Wesleyan movement and its hymns. Hundreds of Charles Wesley's hymns were circulated in Methodist hymnals, including 486 of them in the 1780 *Collection of Hymns for the People Called Methodist,* the one that became the standard for generations. His legacy has never really faded; the 1904 *English Methodist Hymn Book* has 440 of his hymns of its 980 in total. Early Wesleyan testimonial hymns such as "And can it be that I should gain?" were especially popular in the United States. Besides those mentioned already, "Come, Thou Long Expected Jesus" (ELW 254 and LSB 338) and "Jesus Christ is Risen Today" (ELW 365 and LSB 457) are standard Advent and Easter hymns, respectively, and dozens more could be named.[7] Other early Methodists also wrote enduring hymns, such as "All Hail the Power of Jesus' Name" (ELW 634 and LSB 549) by Edward Perronet, the French Huguenot whose itinerant Wesleyan preaching career began in 1746. Such hymns were eventually sung in regular church services and in special revival meetings of all kinds, including the Great Awakening in North America. Fanny Crosby knew them well and added her own prolific poetic output to this strand of hymnody. In recent years, some of Charles Wesley's hymns, including "Love Divine," have been "retuned," namely, adapted not only textually but also musically for twenty-first-century use.[8] The Charles Wesley Society (http://www.wesleysociety.org) has avidly tended his legacy, one that now firmly connects Christian communities across various confessional barriers.

---

7   Such as "Christ the Lord is Risen Today" (ELW 373 and LSB 469); "Christ Whose Glory" (ELW 553 and LSB 873); "Lo, He Comes" (ELW 435 and LSB 336), "You Servants of God" (ELW 825).

8   Bruce H. Benedict and Lester Ruth, "Retuned Hymn Movement," *Hymns and Hymnody,* vol. 3, 308.

10

AMERICAN REVIVALS AND THE SOCIAL GOSPEL (1800–1950)

"This is my story, this is my song"

AS MENTIONED, THE Wesley brothers themselves visited the American colonies, albeit briefly, and their movement sent many more missionaries and hymns there as the colonies became the United States. Isaac Watts had already supplied hymns that found a home here; immigrants like the Moravians and others, Germans but also the Scandinavians, were bringing their hymns to the frontier as well. The nineteenth century saw "Awakenings" and revivals of all sorts, such as Dwight Moody's major gatherings where Christians of many kinds sang the same hymns. Through it all ran the Wesleyan sort of "holiness" represented here by the hymns of Fanny Crosby and her associates.

The western world of Europe and North America had changed in the late eighteenth century, and changed in a way that helps frame these religious revivals. With the Enlightenment push for reason rather than revelation, public life and some official governments became less tied to church teachings, as seen quite dramatically in the French Revolution, but also in other related developments. Insofar as governments and the public sphere became less explicitly Christian, being a committed believer started to mean for many people a more personal experience: individualized, interior, and often intense. Thus arose the age of conversions, revivals, and personal testimonies, especially in the United States.

Revivalism: Fanny Crosby (1820–1915)

Fanny Crosby

English Wesleyans sang a lot, and even sang about the gift of singing, as we have seen. But it was an American Wesleyan woman who captured that sentiment forever: "This is my story; this is my song." Born in 1820 and blind from infancy, Fanny Crosby developed an ear for poetry and eventually devoted it to the music of Christian revival meetings and the Sunday School movement. Her extended family included later a distant cousin known for his singing, namely, Bing, but her own special contributions were in the spoken word, especially in recitals of her poems as taken down by others for posterity. Many of them became hymns, several in wide use today.

Crosby's family came from Boston Puritan stock, and her earliest church affiliations were Presbyterian and Methodist. After a home education when her grandmother and mother would daily read to her the biblical cadences plus the hymns of Watts and Bunyan's *Pilgrim's Progress*, she left home as a talented teenager for Manhattan's Institute for the Blind. There her ability to compose verse spontaneously for any occasion made her the school poet, including tours in upstate New York and with patriotic poems in Washington, D.C. In her mid-twenties she stayed on as one of the school's teachers and became immersed in the Rescue Mission work in Manhattan. With an ear for music, she played piano, organ, harp, and guitar, and became the pianist at the 18th Street Methodist Church in New York.

Upon hearing Isaac Watts's "Alas! And Did My Savior Bleed" (ELW 337 and LSB 437) at a Methodist revival meeting on November 20, 1850, at the 30th Street Methodist Church, she felt her soul "flooded with celestial light." Ever after, she devoted her poetic output to sacred song. Henry Ward Beecher, the Brooklyn Congregationalist, and Phoebe Palmer, the Methodist hostess of Holiness meetings, introduced Fanny to a larger world of church life and music publishing, including the enterprising editor William Bradbury. Her verses then graced multiple hymnals, especially for revival meetings and for Bradbury's Sunday School hymnals. Further, William Howard Doane regularly asked Crosby for texts for his hymnals of "Gospel Songs," including the popular "Safe in the Arms of Jesus" and "Jesus, Keep Me Near the Cross," still in hymnals today (ELW 335).[1] When Phoebe Palmer Knapp brought Crosby a melody and asked for a text, the result was "Blessed Assurance," perhaps her best-known work.

"Blessed Assurance" (ELW 638)

That day in 1873, Phoebe Palmer Knapp, the musical daughter of Methodist Holiness leader Phoebe Palmer, came to visit Fanny Crosby with a tune in her head. She played it for her friend in the hope that the poet would supply some words. Ever ready with a poem for any occasion or even at the mention of someone's name, Crosby later reflected that specific words came immediately to mind. "Blessed Assurance" sprang to life, and it was an immediate hit. It first appeared on the back

---

1   See also "To God Be the Glory" (*Glory to God* 634), and "Rescue the Perishing" in Routley-Richardson, *Panorama* #402.

cover of *The Guide to Holiness* in 1873, then in multiple hymnbooks starting that same year with John Sweeney's *Gems of Praise* and then the 1875 Methodist (U. S.) Hymnal.

Blessed Assurance

1 Bless-ed as-sur-ance, Je-sus is mine! Oh, what a fore-taste of glo-ry di-vine!
2 Per-fect sub-mis-sion, per-fect de-light, vi-sions of rap-ture now burst on my sight;
3 Per-fect sub-mis-sion, all is at rest; I in my Sav-ior am hap-py and blest,

Heir of sal-va-tion, pur-chase of God, born of his Spir-it, washed in his blood.
an-gels de-scend-ing bring from a-bove ech-oes of mer-cy, whis-pers of love.
watch-ing and wait-ing, look-ing a-bove, filled with his good-ness, lost in his love.

Refrain

This is my sto-ry, this is my song, prais-ing my Sav-ior all the day long:

this is my sto-ry, this is my song, prais-ing my Sav-ior all the day long.

Text: Fanny J. Crosby, 1820–1915
Music: ASSURANCE, Phoebe P. Knapp, 1830–1908

Only three stanzas long, the text-tune combination has been remarkably stable, with only the slightest of editing. Crosby's memory bank could quickly arrange rhyming phrases from various sources into a steady rhythm, as evident throughout her life. In this case, what sprang to mind was the first phrase, "blessed assurance," and the rest flowed from there. Let others worry whether they are among the elect or not. This Wesleyan daughter celebrated the firm assurance of salvation, and did so with joy, delight, and even rapture. "Blessed assurance, Jesus is mine! Oh, what a foretaste of glory divine! Heir of salvation, purchase of God, born of his Spirit, washed in his blood." The original read "purchased" of God, the only textual change noted. Otherwise, familiar concepts added up to a fervent expression of faith. "A foretaste of glory divine" echoes the Wesleyan expectations of perfect (complete) holiness, even rapture, as in the second stanza. "Perfect submission, perfect delight, visions of rapture now burst on my sight; angels descending bring from above, echoes of mercy, whispers of love." "Visions" and "sight" may seem to be surprising themes from a blind poet, but not in this case. After all, as Frances Havergal, herself a composer and the author of the familiar consecration hymn "Take My Life and Let it Be," said of Crosby, "Her heart can see."[2]

It was the testimony in the chorus that especially commended this hymn to singers in pews and tents and for singing generations to come. "This is my story, this is my song, praising my Savior all the day long." The last stanza carries special echoes of the Methodist Holiness movement and even of Charles Wesley's "Love Divine": "Perfect submission, all is at rest; I in my savior am happy and blest, Watching and waiting, looking above, filled with his goodness, lost in his love." The themes of perfect submission and rest reflect the "second rest" of the

---

2   For more on this hymn and Crosby's life in general, including her marriage, see Edith Blumhofer, *Her Heart Can See: The Life and Hymns of Fanny J. Crosby* (Grand Rapids, MI: Eerdmans, 2005), here 212. To be cited as Blumhofer, *Crosby*. Further on Havergal's hymns: "Take My Life" in ELW 583 and 685, and LSB 783–84. See also her "Lord, Speak to Us" (ELW 676).

Wesleyan tradition, and "lost in his love" could well have come from Crosby's many years of singing "lost in wonder, love, and praise," the phrase in "Love Divine" that Charles Wesley himself had borrowed from Joseph Addison.

From the 1875 Methodist Hymnal, "Blessed Assurance" spread to Ira Sankey's *Gospel Hymns* in 1887, the Disciples of Christ hymnal in 1888, and the Methodist Hymnal in Canada in 1889. It appeared in twenty more hymnals by the end of the century, and many more thereafter, including African American song books. Attempts to adapt or alter it, such as the 1987 Psalter Hymnal, have never caught on. Dwight Moody, with the equally industrious Ira Sankey at the keyboard, made "Blessed Assurance" a staple at his international revival meetings. In the German translation edited by Walter Rauschenbusch, it was sung as *Sel'ge Gewissheit, Jesus ist mein!* (#339 in his 1897 hymnal), another example of cross-cultural translation.

In general, Crosby's several collaborators were themselves significant sources of American evangelical hymnody. Her partner on this hymn, Phoebe Knapp, wrote hundreds of gospel tunes and hymns. Her contemporary Lowell Mason (1792–1872) arranged hymns by Watts ("Joy to the World") and by Charles Wesley ("Oh, for a Thousand Tongues"), and he composed music for "My Faith Looks Up to Thee" (ELW 759 and LSB 702) and for Watts's "When I Survey the Wondrous Cross" (ELW 803 and LSB 425). Crosby's friend Robert Lowry (1826–99), already mentioned for working with "We're Marching to Zion," supplied text and tune for "Shall We Gather at the River" (ELW 423) and "My Life Flows on in Endless Song" (ELW 763). The latter, an old favorite, supplies the refrain for this whole era: "How can I keep from singing?"

Fanny Crosby's poetry as enshrined in multiple hymns still sung today made her a beloved figure into the twentieth century. She often spoke at New Jersey's famous Ocean Grove meetings, and at Moody's revivals. On Good Friday in 1908 she recited at a Princeton Presbyterian Church while visiting her old friend Grover Cleveland. Her simple, singable texts resonated with the multitudes, for "she sang of faith in an age of doubt, and millions grasped for certainty by joining her song."[3] Composing poetry right to the end at 95 years old, she died in February of 1915 and was buried in Bridgeport, Connecticut, not far from her childhood home. In 1955 a new gravestone was laid, with the first stanza of "Blessed Assurance" on it.

Crosby's career represents an important aspect of American Christianity in the nineteenth century. Her roots were in Wesleyan Holiness soil and her fruits in the trend toward a generic Protestant-ism. Her own experiences of Presbyterian, Congregationalist, and Methodist churches blended together in ways appreciated by hymn singers of many denominations ever since. As with the "Awakening" or revival movement in general, this broad Protestant phenomenon with its shared culture including hymnody was a forerunner of the *non*-denominational future of American Christianity. The stage was set for the ecumenical development of the mid-twentieth century, with its explicit agreements and arrangements. Still, as a successor here to Charles Wesley, Fanny Crosby, with her assurance and warm heart, "this child of the Puritans, pillar of the Sunday School and gos-pel troubadour extraordinaire was, after all, a Methodist."[4] Here, too, Crosby's hymns are not only sung today much as when first heard but also "re-tuned," in this case by Amanda Noel, as part of the "Retuned Hymn Movement."[5]

The Social Gospel, from Rauschenbusch to Fosdick

As evident in Franny Crosby's commitments to New York's Res-cue Missions, the nineteenth century saw a big increase in America's urban poverty and social problems, along with a rapidly expanding

---

3   Blumhofer, *Crosby*, 253.

4   Blumhofer, *Crosby*, 341, in conclusion.

5   Bruce H. Benedict and Lester Ruth, "Retuned Hymn Movement," *Hymns and Hymnody*, vol. 3, 308, n. 18.

immigrant population. Many organizations coupled Christian convictions with personal relief measures, as exemplified by the emergence of the Salvation Army around 1870. Free meals went hand-in-hand with conversions, and all aimed at the individual cases, not the societal causes. Yet the sheer scale of need soon prompted some to speak, write, and advocate for a more structural approach, a "social Christianity." Leaders like preacher Washington Gladden, author Josiah Strong, and economist Richard Ely raised awareness of the societal context, specifically, the institutional forces that led to poverty and hunger for so many. Soon, labor unions and "Christian socialism" were widely debated. The key figure in the pastoral and theological development of the "Social Gospel" was Walter Rauschenbusch (1861–1918), the son of a German Pietist pastor turned American Baptist. Hymnody intersects the story of Rauschenbusch and his legacy in several different ways, although he himself, deaf at thirty years old, could not fully experience the actual singing.

In five generations of German (Westphalian) Lutheran pastors, the Rauschenbusch family cherished the familiar Pietist hymns, but once in the United States they did not share the Lutheran confession.

Walter Rauschenbusch

When Walter became the pastor of the "Second German Baptist Church of New York," near Hell's Kitchen, he saw two pressing needs, both involving hymns. The German congregation needed more hymns in general, and the social context called for more pertinent hymns, in particular. Early on, he addressed the first need by drawing on the Wesleyan Holiness successes of Ocean Grove meetings, including Fanny Crosby's hymns and others published by Dwight Moody's cohort Ira Sankey. At the start of his writing career, Rauschenbusch teamed up with Sankey to expand German-language hymnody by translating dozens of these revival songs himself, recruiting other translators for more, and publishing the results in large hymnals. "What a Friend We Have in Jesus" (ELW 742, LSB 770) became *Welch ein treuer Freund ist Iesus* (by A. Flammer, #27 in the 1897 hymnal combining two earlier ones). Rauschenbusch himself translated "I Need Thee Every Hour" (*Ich brauch' dich allezeit*, #38) and Fanny Crosby's "Draw me nearer" (#56) and her "To the Work" (#60). He had a colleague translate her "Blessed Assurance," as mentioned: *Sel'ge Gewissheit: Jesus ist mein!* (#339, by W. Appel). Again, hymn singing crossed confessional traditions and languages.

Gradually, Rauschenbusch's experience of tenement poverty and his parishioners' desperation led him to realize that individual conversion was not enough. The kingdom of God had social implications. Drawing on his preaching of Jesus's teachings in the Gospels and his reading of other authors, he wrote *Christianity and the Social Crisis* in 1907, to immediate acclaim. He called upon the Old Testament prophets and the social aims of Jesus, all coming now as the kingdom of God. He was not a member of the Socialist Party, but a Pietist applying conversion and regeneration to the social context. "We want not only social service, but social repentance; we want social reform; we want social conversion; we want social regeneration."[6] Even as he

---

6   Christopher H. Evans, *"The Kingdom is Always but Coming": A Life of Walter Rauschenbusch* (Grand Rapids, MI: Eerdmans, 2004), 245. To be cited as Evans, *Rauschenbusch*.

became a famous author and speaker on this theme, Pastor Rauschenbusch still thought about local congregations singing hymns. Such
social convictions needed to take hold at the grassroots level, but traditional hymnody was not attuned to the moment or the emerging
movement. Although he himself wrote occasional poetry, along with
plays and short stories, he never tried his own hand at such hymns, but
he lamented their absence. "We need hymns that will voice the new
social enthusiasm. The old-fashioned hymnals are almost bare of such
material."[7]

Perhaps Rauschenbusch knew that Gladden wrote "O Master, Let Me Walk with You" (ELW 818). He may have known Frank
North's 1903 hymn "Where Cross the Crowded Ways" (ELW 719),
and especially about the hymn's urban social context, since they
corresponded on several related topics. Or perhaps he knew Henry
Sloane Coffin's 1909–10 *Hymns of the Kingdom of God* or Mabel
Mussey's *Social Hymns of Brotherhood and Aspiration*. But as his own
years advanced and his health declined, what he proposed for his
own funeral were the old Pietist classics cherished by his father and
grandfather: Paul Gerhardt's "Commit Your Ways to God" (tr. John
Wesley), G. Tersteegen's "I Worship the Power of Love," and G. Voi-
ghtländer's "Under the Lilies Come Every Joy." Just as it may seem
incongruous to cite a German version of "Blessed Assurance" from
the 1890s, so too the naming of these German hymns in their rare
English translations may seem out of place. But in 1918, the year of
Rauschenbusch's death, World War I had forced many German American congregations to use English only and to do so in a hurry.[8] For
a hymn that represents the Social Gospel more fully, we can turn to
an admirer of Rauschenbusch, Harry Emerson Fosdick. His "God of
Grace and God of Glory" was written for the 1930 opening and 1931

---

7 Evans, *Rauschenbusch*, 224.

8 Evans, *Rauschenbusch,* 247.

dedication of Riverside Church in New York City, itself an enduring twentieth-century monument to the same movement.

Harry Emerson Fosdick (1878–1969)

Harry Emerson Fosdick

The devastation of the Great War also damaged the optimism of liberal Christianity and thus the Social Gospel movement. Progress in human affairs was not so evident, and hopes for the coming kingdom of God had to be tempered. Yet the social dimension of Christianity as championed by Rauschenbusch remained central to American churches after the war, as also seen in inter-church developments such as the Federal Council of Churches, the forerunner of the National Council of Churches. In fact, the early phases of the modern ecumenical movement often featured social statements and shared societal endeavors, along with shared hymns. Churches that could not agree on doctrinal details could cooperate on good causes like peace and justice, and could sing together about them. Harry Emerson Fosdick, raised and educated in such a context, became its most visible representative as the preacher/author of the new nondenominational and "progressive" Riverside Church in New York City.[9] And, he wrote hymns, one of them still sung and quite expressive of these developments, namely, "God of Grace and God of Glory."

Fosdick's career follows that of Rauschenbusch in several ways, as he himself points out in his autobiography bearing a title taken from his famous hymn, *The Living of These Days.* They both came from upstate New York Baptist families and undergraduate education, and were both deeply influenced by their experiences amid the social desperation in Manhattan's poorest neighborhoods. Fosdick's student years at Union Theological Seminary (1900–04) meant reading predecessors like Washington Gladden, and his first preaching call coincided with Rauschenbusch's breakthrough book, *Christianity and the Social Crisis* (1907). Fosdick's memoir makes warm personal reference to Rauschenbusch: "I was strongly influenced by him. He was an inspiriting person to meet."[10] For the fiftieth anniversary of that book in 1957, *A Rauschenbusch Reader* featured "An Interpretation of the Life and Work of Walter Rauschenbusch" by Fosdick himself, who was then looking back on his own career from retirement a decade earlier in 1948. Here, as in the autobiography, Fosdick documents his admiration for and continuation of Rauschenbusch's program: "personal and social Christianity were blended; they were one gospel indivisible. . . . Personal rebirth and social rebirth are inseparably necessary. One involves the other."[11] Apparently, the admiration was mutual. In 1914

---

9   Robert M. Miller, *Harry Emerson Fosdick: Preacher, Pastor, Prophet* (New York: Oxford University Press, 1985).

10   "Inspiriting" is Fosdick's own word in his autobiography; H. E. Fosdick, *The Living of These Days: An Autobiography* (New York: Harper and Row, 1956), 109. To be cited as Fosdick, *Living.*

11   *A Rauschenbusch Reader: The Kingdom of God and the Social Gospel,* compiled by Benson Y. Landis (New York: Harper, 1957), xvii and xix. See also William Lee Pitts, *The Reception of Rauschenbusch* (Macon, GA: Mercer University Press, 2018), 311–312, 319–320, 329.

the old Professor Rauschenbusch had named young Pastor Fosdick, also at that time a preaching instructor at Union Seminary, among his nominees to become president of his seminary in Rochester.[12]

"God of Grace and God of Glory" (ELW 705, LSB 850)

Fosdick's energies and rhetorical gifts in the pulpit, over the radio, and on the printed page (eventually in dozens of books) led him to more and more prominence and controversy as pastor and seminary professor, and even to the cover of *Time* magazine. Just the title of a famous sermon indicates his polemical context: "Must the Fundamentalists Win?" The pinnacle of his career was the big new, non-credal and nondenominational church called Riverside. The building's opening service on October 5, 1930, and its dedication in February of 1931 both featured the hymn that the preacher wrote for the occasion. Three other hymn texts from his prolific pen also survive, one for his cherished peace movement ("The Prince of Peace his Banner Spreads") and another he thought "deeper" in meaning than his famous one, "O God in Restless Living."[13] Only "God of Grace and God of Glory," however, has become widely used. He called it "a very personal prayer on my part,"[14] and it has come to stand for a "peace and justice" Christianity in countless hymnals. It was originally five stanzas long and set to a different melody than later, namely, REGENT SQUARE, as in "Angels from the Realms of Glory." Erik Routley claimed that Fosdick "deplored" the way the Methodists had paired his text with CWM RHONDDA, also "Guide me ever, great Redeemer/Jehovah," a pairing that has endured.[15]

Some of Fosdick's phrases have rung true of different social causes across many generations: "Grant us wisdom, grant us courage, for the facing of this hour, . . . for the living of these days." "Warring

---

12 Evans, *Rauschenbusch,* 257.

13 Fosdick, *Living,* 210.

14 Fosdick, *Living,* 209.

15 Routley-Richardson, *Panorama,* p. 433.

God of Grace and God of Glory

1 God of grace and God of glo - ry, on your peo - ple
2 Lo! The hosts of e - vil round us scorn the Christ, as -
3 Cure your chil - dren's war - ring mad - ness; bend our pride to
4 Save us from weak res - ig - na - tion to the e - vils

pour your pow'r; crown your an - cient chur - ch's sto - ry;
sail his ways! From the fears that long have bound us
your con - trol; shame our wan - ton, self - ish glad - ness,
we de - plore; let the gift of your sal - va - tion

bring its bud to glo - rious flow'r. Grant us wis - dom, grant us cour - age
free our hearts to faith and praise. Grant us wis - dom, grant us cour - age
rich in things and poor in soul. Grant us wis - dom, grant us cour - age,
be our glo - ry ev - er - more. Grant us wis - dom, grant us cour - age,

for the fac - ing of this hour, for the fac - ing of this hour.
for the liv - ing of these days, for the liv - ing of these days.
lest we miss your king - dom's goal, lest we miss your king - dom's goal.
serv - ing you whom we a - dore, serv - ing you whom we a - dore.

Text: Harry E. Fosdick, 1878–1969
Music: CWM RHONDDA, John Hughes, 1873–1932

madness" and "wanton, selfish gladness, rich in things and poor in soul" can be called out in any age, but remnants of the Social Gospel's more specific wording echo here too, especially "your kingdom's goal" and the implied optimism in the oft-omitted (fourth) stanza: "Set our feet on lofty places; Gird our lives that they may be/ Armored with all Christlike graces/ In the fight to set men free. Grant us wisdom, Grant us courage, /That we fail not men nor thee." Perhaps a textual change in the final stanza also reflects a turn from human striving to divine giving. Fosdick had written "Let the search for thy salvation be our glory evermore" whereas modern hymnals often read "Let the gift of your salvation."

Fosdick's hymns were appended to the hymnal in use at Riverside Church, namely, *Hymns for the Living Age*, 1923, edited by H. Augustine Smith, which already contained many hymns of brotherhood, justice, social progress, and world peace.[16] They were often sung there, especially this one, including at his funeral, and became well known.

Riverside Church came to represent the twentieth century's non-denominational, social justice type of church, including pacifist and civil rights causes well past Fosdick's tenure there. Among many others, Martin Luther King Jr., preached at Riverside and paid tribute to Fosdick's own preaching.[17] "God of Grace and God of Glory" can stand for the Social Gospel movement as it evolved in the full twentieth century, including the Civil Rights movement, but African Americans also had their own traditions of singing.

---

16 Specifically, "God of Grace and God of Glory" was taken from *Praise and Service* #242, ed. H. Augustine Smith (New York: Century, 1932) to become 534 in the appendix to Riverside's hymnal, *Hymns for the Living Age*. "The Prince of Peace" #329 became 535, and "O God in Restless Living" #210 became 536. *Praise and Service* also included a large section of "Responsive Readings Selected and Arranged by H. E. F." [Fosdick himself] 374–416.

17 Fosdick, *Living*, 335.

11

AFRICAN AMERICAN HYMNODY (1800–)

"Sing a song"

ONE MAN'S PERSONAL heartache ("I am tired, I am weak, I am worn") can resonate with others who have never heard Thomas Dorsey's story. But how do those whose families have never known slavery share lines from "Lift Every Voice and Sing" like "Stony the road we trod, bitter the chast'ning rod"? Such songs can help us to glimpse, and perhaps somehow even to share, the concrete experiences of others, but always with respect for some unique contexts. The cruel rod of actual slavery should give the reader pause as it does the historian.

African American songs also provide an excellent example of non-denominational hymnody; they came from several sources and have gone out to Christian hymnals across the denominational spectrum. As with other movements or groups, it is presumptuous to describe the Black Church and its music in such a brief way and with only a few samples. For one thing, not all Black churches were or are alike. There were hymnals for some organized groups such as the African Methodist Episcopal Church and AME Zion. Within the AME context, for example, Richard Allen's *Collection of Spiritual Songs and Hymns, Selected from Various Authors* (1801) was followed by an 1818 hymnal with 314 hymns, many from the Watts/Wesley tradition.[1]

But there are also two contrasting examples of song types, originally not in hymnals at all, that stand out. First, the "spirituals," once called *American Negro Spirituals* (a collection to be quoted shortly), were

---

1   Michael W. Harris, *The Rise of Gospel Blues: The Music of Thomas Andrew Dorsey in the Urban Church* (New York: Oxford University Press, 1992), 7. To be cited as Harris, *Dorsey*.

widely sung before and after the Civil War, and then gradually became familiar around the world. With a rhythmic "call and response" parallel to some preaching styles, and especially the Old Testament theme of liberation or deliverance, these songs were and are well known without needing hymnals or instrumental accompaniment. Consider "Swing low sweet chariot, Comin' for to carry me home," or "Go down, Moses, 'Way down in Egypt land, Tell ole Pharoah, To let my people go."[2] Second, a specific and quite different example of choral music also stands out, not a "spiritual" but what the NAACP around 1919 designated as its official anthem, namely, "Lift Every Voice and Sing," often called the "Black National Anthem." Preservation of the spirituals and the creation of "Lift Every Voice and Sing" are both the shared work of two brothers.

James Weldon Johnson (1871–1938) and J. Rosamond Johnson (1873–1954)

James Weldon Johnson

---

2   *The Books of American Negro Spirituals*, edited with introduction by James Weldon Johnson, musical arrangements by J. Rosamond Johnson (New York: Viking Press, 1969; Da Capo paperback reprint 1977), originally two volumes: *The Book of American Negro Spirituals* in 1925 and *The Second Book of Negro Spirituals* in 1926. To be cited as *Spirituals* i and ii; in this case, i, 62 and 51.

"Lift Every Voice and Sing" (1900; ELW 841, LSB 964)

In poetry of a complex texture and with a challenging tune and wide vocal range, "Lift Every Voice and Sing" is rightly called an anthem rather than a hymn. It was originally written not for church use but for a large public school chorus at a national anniversary in 1900. "Sing a song" full of faith and hope, the Johnson brothers wrote. Ever since, it has been sung at school assemblies, national anniversaries, local pageants, and civil rights rallies, along with gradual inclusion in hymnals for congregational use. In its original context at the end of the nineteenth century, the "chast'ning rod" was a bitter reminder of the very recent violence of widespread slavery and "the blood of the slaughtered." The reminder should be no less provocative in the twenty-first century. Phrases from the anthem have populated book titles and political speeches across a secular spectrum, and its third stanza is plainly a prayer.

> *God of our weary years, God of our silent tears, thou*
> *who hast brought us thus far on the way; thou who hast*
> *by thy might led us into the light, keep us forever in the*
> *path, we pray. Lest our feet stray from the places, our*
> *God, where we met thee; lest, our hearts drunk with*
> *the wine of the world, we forget thee; shadowed beneath*
> *thy hand, may we forever stand, true to our God, true*
> *to our native land.*

As different as the spirituals and "Lift Every Voice" are in words, music, and usage, their stories can be told together. They share basic themes, of course. More specifically, the creators of "Lift Every Voice and Sing" were also the editors, arrangers, and advocates of *The Books of American Negro Spirituals* (1925 and 1926), as they called their collections. Two brothers, poet James Weldon Johnson and musician J. Rosamond Johnson, first created the anthem and then compiled two collections of spirituals. Their stories can guide us into this rich topic.

Lift Every Voice and Sing

1 Lift ev - 'ry voice and sing till earth and heav - en ring,
2 Ston - y the road we trod, bit - ter the chas - t'ning rod,
3 God of our wea - ry years, God of our si - lent tears,

ring with the har - mo - nies of lib - er - ty.
felt in the days when hope un - born had died;
thou who hast brought us thus far on the way;

Let our re - joic - ing rise high as the lis - t'ning skies,
yet with a stead - y beat, have not our wea - ry feet
thou who hast by thy might led us in - to the light,

let it re - sound loud as the roll - ing sea.
come to the place for which our par - ents sighed?
keep us for - ev - er in the path, we pray.

Sing a song full of the faith that the dark past has taught us;
sing a song full of the hope that the pres - ent has brought us;
fac - ing the ris - ing sun of our new day be - gun,
let us march on till vic - to - ry is won.

We have come o - ver a way that with tears has been wa - tered;
we have come, tread-ing our path through the blood of the slaugh - tered,
out from the gloom - y past, till now we stand at last
where the white gleam of our bright star is cast.

Lest our feet stray from the plac - es, our God, where we met thee;
lest, our hearts drunk with the wine of the world, we for-get thee;
shad-owed be - neath thy hand, may we for - ev - er stand,
true to our God, true to our na - tive land.

Text: James W. Johnson, 1871–1938
Music: LIFT EVERY VOICE AND SING, J. Rosamond Johnson, 1873–1954

J. Rosamond Johnson

James and J. Rosamond Johnson were well-educated, starting in a strong public school system in Jacksonville, Florida, where their Bahamian-Haitian mother was their first teacher. From the Stanton School for Negroes, James the poet went on to Atlanta University, reading Rudyard Kipling for example, and Rosamond the composer went to the New England Conservatory and then to London. When James returned to Florida as the principal of the Stanton School, his brother was nearby at the Florida Baptist Academy. For Lincoln's birthday in 1900, James wrote a poem, Rosamond the music, and five hundred school children first did and sang what the title says, "Lift Every Voice and Sing." It was dedicated to Booker T. Washington, leader of educational programs such as his Tuskegee Institute. With its stirring melody and frank text about a dark past yet hope for victory, their work caught on in other schools as well. James used color language freely, such as "dark" or the "white gleam of our bright star." An article about the Johnson brothers and their "anthem," as it was quickly called, spread the word in 1901 in a strategic monthly, *Colored American.*[3] From there, "Lift Every Voice" spread rapidly and became a standard for schools, pageants, and African American gatherings such as Emancipation Day, the birth-day of Frederick Douglass, and Juneteenth. The NAACP declared it their official song, distributing copies widely and naming James Weldon Johnson as Executive Secretary, a leadership role he held from 1920 to 1930. Through the twentieth century, the anthem maintained a prominent place in public gatherings small and large, as well as church services.

From the Historic Black Colleges and Universities and Paul Robeson to Martin Luther King's speeches, Black Power, and in Joseph Lowry's benediction at Barack Obama's first presidential inauguration, "Lift Every Voice and Sing" has been a consistent feature of African American solidarity.[4] Even when the simpler "We Shall Overcome" became more popular during the Civil Rights movement, the anthem remained strong in church life and was thus used and cherished by new generations.[5] After all, the struggle continued and "let us march on" looked ever ahead. Books like *Stony the Road* (both the recent one by Henry Louis Gates, and the earlier one by Cain Felder with its 30th anniversary edition in 2021) and *May We Forever Stand* by Imani Perry testify in their very titles to its staying power. Demonstrating that words from one historical context can apply to others, the voting rights campaign in Joseph Biden's 2021 presidential administration carried the title "Lift every voice."

---

3   Edited by Victoria Mathews. The *LSB Companion* 964 cites a 1900 publication of the anthem by Joseph W. Stern in New York City, no. 3071–73.

4   Including a Chicago Bulls game on February 4, 1986; see Imani Perry, *May We Forever Stand: A History of the Black National Anthem* (Chapel Hill, NC: The University of North Carolina Press, 2018), 203–204. To be cited as Perry, *Anthem.* "Lift Every Voice" was also part of the pregame program at the Super Bowl on February 12, 2023.

5   Perry, *Anthem,* 89.

The Spirituals

Alongside this anthem, the spirituals were also preserved through oral tradition and community use, even when some Black church leaders preferred "traditional" (white) hymnody for church services. After the Civil War, these simple songs, often in a distinctive dialect, struck some as too primitive, too tied to slavery's past, and some prominent figures like AME bishop Daniel Payne worked to replace them with hymns he considered more stately and literary.[6] Yet even such a literate poet and authority as James Weldon Johnson himself recognized the "miracle of the spirituals."[7] The poetic tribute that opens his Preface to *The Books of American Negro Spirituals* has been cited often: "O black and unknown bards of long ago, How came your lips to touch the sacred fire?" The volumes extol the simple power of their pulsing rhythm and liberating refrains. Ignoring "Lift Every Voice," the Johnson brothers' collections drew on oral tradition to supply over a hundred examples of spirituals, some of them widely known and sung today.

Current Lutheran hymnals include multiple spirituals, a baker's dozen in *Evangelical Lutheran Worship* (the ELW), with some texts matching the Johnson collection. Two examples are "Give me Jesus" and "My Lord, What a Mornin' " (ELW 770, LSB 976, *Spirituals* i, 160–161; ELW 438, LSB 968, *Spirituals,* i, 162–163). Good Friday is especially well represented. Entitled "Crucifixion" in the first Johnson collection, "They crucified my Lord" (ELW 350) is known for its refrain "an' He never said a mumbalin' word" (*Spirituals* i, 174–176). Better known is "Were You There When They Crucified My Lord?" The five stanzas of ELW 353 match exactly the Johnsons' *Second Book of Negro Spirituals* (*Spirituals,* ii, 136–137) whereas LSB 456 uses three of those original stanzas and adds "Were you there when God raised Him from the tomb?" Widely sung as a communion hymn is "Let Us Break Bread Together" (ELW 471), originally "When I Fall On My

---

6   Harris, *Dorsey,* 3, on "ring" shouts.
7   *Spirituals,* i, 15.

Knees (Wid My Face to de Risin' Sun)" in the *Second Book* (*Spirituals*, ii, 63–65). There are dozens more still in use today, as seen in many other hymnals.[8]

James Weldon Johnson not only edited and thus documented these common texts; he also championed their value over against more formal choral numbers with their elite choirs and organs.

> *I have said that these songs passed through a period when the front ranks of the Negro race would have been willing to let them die. Immediately following Emancipation those ranks revolted against everything connected with slavery, and among those things were the Spirituals. It became a sign of not being progressive or educated to sing them. This was a natural reaction, but, nevertheless, a sadly foolish one. It was left for the older generation to keep them alive by singing them at prayer meetings, class meetings, experience meetings and revivals, while the new choir with the organ and books of idiotic anthems held sway on Sundays.*[9]

Just as later congregational use kept "Lift Every Voice" in singing circulation, so here the early prayer meetings and revivals had kept the spirituals in use even when Sunday morning did not. As Johnson and others have since documented in full, it was also the Historic Black Colleges and Universities, starting with the Fisk choirs, that preserved the spirituals in their concert form and brought them to a larger public, indeed to global fame in the twentieth century. Dr. King closed his "I Have a Dream" speech "in the words of the old Negro Spiritual: 'Free at last,' " also in the Johnson brothers' collection (*Spirituals*, ii, 158–159).

---

8   See especially *This Far by Faith: An African American Resource for Worship* (Minneapolis: Augsburg Fortress, 1999) and *African American Heritage Hymnal* (Chicago: GIA Publications, 2001).

9   *Spirituals*, i, 49.

Thomas A. Dorsey (1899–1993)

The story of singing in the Black Church needs one more example, beyond the nineteenth-century spirituals as revived later and the 1900 school song that became a powerful anthem to this day. In the twentieth century the "blues" and "gospel jazz" music arose and flourished in general, and specifically the "gospel blues" of Thomas A. Dorsey. "Precious Lord, Take My Hand" represents his tumultuous year of success and tragedy in 1932, and lives on in diverse hymnals around the world.

Thomas A. Dorsey (known as "Georgia Tom" and not "Tommy" Dorsey, the trombone player and band leader) was born in 1899 in Georgia to a preacher-sharecropper father and a devout piano-playing mother. For decades he oscillated between his musical gifts as expressed in bars and night life, and his church activity, including Sunday mornings. Church singing in his youth was a mixture of "slave spirituals, the white Protestant hymns, and shaped note music," plus a type of improvised "moaning" that showed up later in

Thomas A. Dorsey, at Ma Rainey's right hand

the blues.[10] Moving north, with thousands of others, Dorsey's musical talent flourished in Chicago. In 1923 he composed and copyrighted some songs, and reconnected with an Atlanta singer, Bessie Smith. A year later he was pianist and leader of the Wild Cats Jazz Band with "Ma" Rainey, and thus became famous on the Saturday night side of his life.

On the church side, the big Chicago congregations at that time exemplified what James Johnson wrote about the opposition of the new choirs and organ over against the slave spirituals. Proper music meant not just staid white Protestant hymns (Watts, Charles Wesley and company) but also choir anthems and concerts of Handel and Mendelssohn.[11] Prominent Black Churches like J. C. Austin's Pilgrim Baptist Church in Chicago performed Mozart's *Ave Verum* and Haydn's *Creation,* with orchestra. (As for performing and perhaps imitating classical music on the European model, a famous Czech composer, Antonin Dvořak [1841–1904], pointed out during his trek to the New World that Americans had a rich reservoir of their own traditional music to draw upon for inspiration, namely, Native American and African American music. Only recently has this advice registered with composers and orchestras enough to become part of classical concert programming.) Alongside the more formal music, Thomas Dorsey's bluesy arrangements and leadership of a "gospel chorus" in 1931 over at Ebenezer Baptist Church under the Rev. J. H. L. Smith met a need too, but not on Sunday mornings when the formal "senior choir" held sway. Blues and jazz were not easily welcomed in official church worship. There were other occasions, including alternative church meetings, for this other kind of music.

---

10   Harris, *Dorsey,* 22.

11   Harris, *Dorsey,* 106–108. See also Kira Thurman, *Singing Like Germans: Black Musicians in the Land of Bach, Beethoven, and Brahms* (Ithaca, NY: Cornell University Press, 2021).

When Dr. Austin invited Ebenezer's Gospel Chorus to Pilgrim Baptist Church in February of 1932, Dorsey's flashy piano and his chorus's energetic "hollers and amens" launched a new day. Dorsey moved to Pilgrim Baptist, his Gospel Chorus there vied with its senior choir, and the "gospel blues" began to replace "proper" European singing. Pilgrim Baptist Church became Dorsey's church home for forty years. Dorsey and his allies were riding a wave and quickly organized a "National Convention of Gospel Choirs and Choruses," including a triumphant concert in August of 1932. The phrase "gospel choir" started to mean a specific type of African American singing.

"Precious Lord, Take My Hand" (ELW 773, LSB 739)

Dorsey's year of triumph, however, quickly turned to tragedy, which also led to his enduring contribution, "Precious Lord." In late August of 1932 his wife died in childbirth and the baby boy too, and his life fell apart. One day the next month, "fumbling around at the keyboard with an old tune,"[12] Dorsey put his own words to that melody: heartache words of woe ("tired, weak, and worn") and frank words of petition ("take my hand, lead me on, lead me home"). In a later interview, he commented on these words from his own experience.

> *Precious Lord, take my hand, lead me on, let me stand. I am tired. [True, I was so tired.] I am weak, I am worn. Through the storm [plenty storm in my life now], through the night [hard night], lead me on to the light. [There had to be a light somewhere. There must be some happiness left somewhere. There must be success somewhere]. Take my hand, precious Lord, lead me on.*[13]

---

12 Apparently, it was George Allen's tune for "Must Jesus Bear the Cross Alone?" in H. W. Beecher's Plymouth Collection hymnal of 1855. Harris, *Dorsey,* 228.

13 ELW 773, LSB 739; for the interview containing the extra phrases, see the *LSB Companion* 739, p. 1049.

Sung immediately at his church, "Precious Lord" took off and was then featured at National Baptist Conventions in New York in 1935 and Los Angeles in 1937, with Dorsey as director and with another Chicago collaborator, Mahalia Jackson, as soloist. Her later career in radio, records, the Civil Rights movement, and prominent concerts ensured its spread beyond the Black Church, as evident in hymnals and popular recordings worldwide. She sang it, for example, at the 1968 funeral of Martin Luther King Jr. Dorsey composed, or at least arranged and published with copyright, hundreds of gospel songs and stayed active until his death in 1993.[14] His 1932 "Precious Lord" lives on as a classic of Black Church singing, alongside the spirituals and "Lift Every Voice and Sing," all shared now with the ecumenical church worldwide. Further, jazz and swing greats like Duke Ellington and Ella Fitzgerald were also expressions of the Black Church and its music, as noted in a recent book with yet another echo of the anthem: *Lift Every Voice and Swing.*[15]

The Song Goes On

The spirituals and the gospel blues live on in the Black Church and in discussions of Black Theology. In 1969 and 1970, respectively, James H. Cone wrote *Black Theology and Black Power* and then *Black Theology of Liberation.* Some Black critics, including Charles Long and his own brother Cecil Wayne Cone, thought that these books were too enamored with theoretical concepts like Black Power and especially too dependent upon white European methods and theologians like Karl Barth, Paul Tillich, and Dietrich Bonhoeffer. They pointed out the author's neglect of the lived experience in Black religious life. In response, James Cone then wrote *The Spirituals and the Blues* in 1972. His autobiographical introduction concluded "*I am the blues*

---

14   For example, "Like a Ship," *This Far by Faith,* 251; "Walking up the King's Highway," *African American Heritage Hymnal,* 402.

15   Vaughn A. Booker, *Lift Every Voice and Swing: Black Musicians and Religious Culture in the Jazz Century* (New York: New York University Press, 2020).

and *my life is a spiritual*" (7). Much later he reflected on this sequence of books. "I wrote *The Spirituals and the Blues* to show that black liberation theology was not, as Long had suggested, derived primarily from the European theology I studied in graduate school."[16]

Finally, just as congregations a century ago debated whether it was proper to admit the world's "blues" music or jazz into church, so too more recently has hip hop or rap challenged the boundaries of church music, and not only in the Black Church. Kurtis Blow, a successful rapper since 1979, became an ordained minister in 2009 and serves the Hip Hop Church of Harlem. On the Lutheran side, Kelly "Glow" Williams, a pastor's daughter, led the singing at Lutheran Youth Gatherings in 2003, 2006, and 2015, the year she received the Gospel Choice Award as "Best Holy Hip Hop Artist."

In the second half of the twentieth century, African American perspectives were expanded by the Anti-Apartheid movement in South Africa, part of the global story of "World Christianity" coming into view.

---

16   James H. Cone, *Said I Wasn't Gonna Tell Nobody* (Maryknoll, New York: Orbis Books, 2018), 95. For Cecil Wayne Cone's perspective, see his *The Identity Crisis in Black Theology* (Nashville, TN: AME Church, 1975), 114–122.

12

WORLD CHRISTIANITY (1950–)

"We are singing in the Light of God"

WHEN CONGREGATIONS TODAY sing "Siyahamba (We are Marching in the Light of God)" they may know that it comes from the
Anti-Apartheid movement in South Africa. But few know that the
song came into English from a Swedish rendition, reflecting a complex
case of cross-cultural, international communication in what is now
called "World Christianity."

Since about 1950, modern Christian history both continued
some trends evident in the earlier twentieth century and also entered a
new era sometimes called "post-modern." Several major aspects of this
period have direct connections to the hymns Christians sing today. In
general, and especially with the explosion of new forms of communication, the world grew smaller. As with music overall, hymns were shared
around the world, sometimes with amazing speed.

As represented earlier by the Social Gospel movement and Harry
Emerson Fosdick in particular, twentieth-century American Christianity saw a rise in inter-denominational or ecumenical cooperation,
especially in the cause of social justice. Examples of "peace and justice"
hymns across denominational lines have made the point. In the late
twentieth century, actions for racial justice in the United States were
linked to a global movement, as seen in the Anti-Apartheid songs from
South Africa.

A worldwide perspective grew throughout the century, from the
1910 World Missionary Conference in Edinburgh naming the goal
of "world evangelization" through multiple examples of ecumenical

cooperation in mission fields around the world, and indeed in the creation of organizations like the World Council of Churches in 1948. Hymns were shared across old confessional boundaries, on the small and local level and at big World Council Assemblies. By the end of the century, this global trend was no longer framed as missions from the northern and colonial powers but as the rise of the global south on its own terms. Thus, this chapter's label: World Christianity.

There is one more mid-century development to keep in mind. Alongside this combination of missionary energies, ecumenical cooperation, and social justice concerns, perhaps the single most influential event in twentieth-century Christian history was the Second Vatican Council (1962–65). However, the category of "event" must be stretched to recognize several months of meetings by thousands of people every autumn for four years. Vatican II, as it is called, was Pope John XXIII's inspiration for a renewal of the church, including the unity of all Christians. Even if structural unity did not result, here or in the ecumenical movement generally, a warmer atmosphere of openness to dialogue and cooperation did. Further, the Council included Commissions on Justice and Peace that matched the era's overall concerns. Many of the Council's topics were specific to Roman Catholic polity and practice, such as the role of bishops and the discipline of fasting. But the most visible and audible result of Vatican II applies to our topic quite directly. Encouraging the use of local languages for worship instead of Latin meant new translations and new musical settings for the *Kyrie,* the *Gloria,* and other components of the Mass. This in turn encouraged translators, poets, and composers to write new hymns for Roman Catholics and then the worldwide church. While the social justice theme is most evident in the South African examples, the impact of Vatican II on contemporary hymnody starts in the Spanish and Latin American context sketched below.

Two other features of twentieth-century Christian history have not yet fully influenced hymnody, at least not for Lutheran congregations: the big Pentecostal movement worldwide and the broad but selective opening of leadership roles to women, including ordination. Those developments are still unfolding.

At the turn into the twenty-first century, the phrase "World Christianity" has expressed the enormous variety in Christian geography, language, culture, and music, and thus enrichment in congregational singing as well.[1] Striving to be neither Eurocentric nor mostly about North American missionaries, World Christianity refers to the many indigenous expressions of postcolonial Christianity flourishing today in Africa, Asia, and Latin America. Some of these communities stem from ancient beginnings, such as Egypt and Ethiopia in Africa, plus parts of India, Iran, and Iraq. In other cases, such as other parts of Africa, all of Latin America and much of East Asia, the starting points may have been modern missionaries from Mediterranean or European contexts or North America, but many communities there have evolved in their own way. Even where such churches have developed self-governance and finance, they have often retained a loyalty to Western hymnody, especially for Sunday morning services. The texts were translated, but the tunes often remained. Alongside that legacy, however, some indigenous local musical expressions have emerged and have gradually become part of hymnals worldwide. In many contexts, the denominational mission fields turned into ecumenical or non-denominational Christian cultures, complete with a mixture of hymn texts and musical styles. Pentecostal movements have added enrichment and further diversity in all these places, albeit with their own heavy debt to Western music.

By very definition, therefore, contemporary World Christianity cannot be represented by a single hymn or two, as attempted here for earlier movements or periods. Rather, the point is exactly in the wide variety of many different songs from widely diverse languages and cultures. What we can notice is that hymns lead the cross-cultural and ecumenical way, as also glimpsed at some meetings of the World

---

1   For literature on World Christianity in general, see *The Journal of World Christianity* (New York Theological Seminary), for example, vol. 11.2 (2021).

Council of Churches, such as Nairobi in 1975 and Vancouver in 1983. It is limiting, but necessary, to focus on what may be known to the readers of this survey, by way of *Evangelical Lutheran Worship* or *All Creation Sings*, for example, and other such resources in English. Several major geographical categories can help organize this abundance of hymnic riches.

Africa

An early and prominent infusion of songs from South Africa came into broad usage with *Freedom is Coming* (1984), conveying in English a musical side to the Anti-Apartheid movement. Ecumenical solidarity with this justice campaign led American choirs and congregations to sing *Siyahamba* in Zulu/Xhosa. "We are Marching in the Light of God" (ELW 866), offers textual variety (marching, dancing, singing, for different stanzas) and harmonic and improvisational possibilities. It quickly became widely known, and other "freedom songs" soon followed. The English text itself has levels of meaning. "We" is communal, of course, and can also include the ancestors; "are marching" means a movement that is united both physically and spiritually; "in the light of God" refers to both a righteous enlightenment in general and also to Christ the light of God in particular.

Freedom is Coming (1984), edited by Anders Nyberg, also supplied other South African "chorus" songs to American Protestant hymnals, including the namesake "Freedom is Coming" (*All Creation Sings* 903). "Hallelujah! We Sing Your Praises; *Haleluya! Pelo tsa rona*" (ELW 535), "Send Me, Jesus; *Thuma mina, Nkosi yam* " (ELW 549 and 809), and others came from the same 1984 source collection and its prior social-political context. To illustrate World Christianity's international reach, these songs were first translated into Swedish and thence, by Gracia Grindal, into English. Further from this context are Desmond Tutu's Pauline prayer set to John Bell's tune ("Goodness is Stronger than Evil," ELW 721), a paraphrase of "Your Will Be Done; *Mayenziwe*" (ELW 741), and, from Zimbabwe, Alexander Gondo's "Come, All You

We Are Marching in the Light of God
Siyahamba

(*Continued*)

Text: South African traditional; tr. *Freedom Is Coming*, 1984
Music: SIYAHAMBA, South African traditional; arr. *Freedom Is Coming*
Tr. and arr. © 1984 Utryck, admin. Walton Music Corp.

People; *Uyaimose*" (ELW 819, also transcribed by I-to Loh for *African Songs of Worship*, 1986). Finally, the congregation sang "Amen, We Praise Your Name; *Amen siakudumisa*" (ELW 846) at Tutu's installation in Capetown in 1986, and the archbishop broke into a dance.

Other African countries are also major sources of songs in wide circulation, including Tanzania, Cameroon, and Ghana. From the Lutheran Theological College in Makumira, Tanzania, with Howard S. Olson (1922–2010) as prolific translator, came "Christ Has Arisen, Alleluia; *Mfurahini, haleluya*" in Swahili by Bernard Kyamanywa (ELW 364 and LSB 466), "Gracious Spirit, Heed our Pleading"; *Njoo kwetu, Roho mwemna* by Wilson Niwagila (ELW 401), and a Kenyan tune "Listen, God is Calling"; *Neno lake Mungu* (ELW 513 and LSB 833). Olson's long career in Tanzania included collecting, editing, translating, and promoting such hybrid hymns, a mixture of African melodies and Western four-part harmony.[2] Cameroon communities have given us "He Came Down" (ELW 253), and a processional that was originally in French, "Praise, Praise, Praise the Lord" (ELW 875). From Ghana came "Jesu, Jesu, Fill Us With Your Love" (ELW 708 and LSB 980, with credit to Tom Colvin), a Kyrie (*With One Voice* 601), and Emmanuel Grantson's "That Priceless Grace" (ELW 591). See also Patrick Matsikenyiri's "Jesus, We Are Gathered; *Jesu, tawa pano*" from Zimbabwe (ELW 529) and his harmonious *Alleluia* (*Glory to God* 590). For good examples of African creativity crossing continents and centuries, see the Swahili variation on St. Francis's "All Creatures of Our God and King" in the anthem "*O Sifuni Mungu*" (arranged by Roger Emerson) and the arrangement by Paul Caldwell and Sean Ivory of "*Thula Sizwe*" with "Of the Father's Love Begotten." As fueled early on by the Western support for the Anti-Apartheid movement in South Africa, the list of African songs in hymnals worldwide grows annually.

Latin America

In broad strokes, the story of Latin American hymnody, first in the original languages and then as translated into many more, is primarily a consequence of Vatican II. When the Roman Catholic Church encouraged translations of the Latin Mass into local tongues, new

---

2   Routley-Richardson, *Panorama*, #922–26, pp. 647–649.

songs were also added to the Mass and to other services. New Spanish and Portuguese texts were sung to traditional and new melodies, and spread to many cultures and contexts as another example of World Christianity. For example, Cesáreo Gabaráin (1936–91) was a Spanish Roman Catholic priest who wrote hundreds of songs, both texts and tunes, especially in the aftermath of Vatican II. His best-known hymn, translated into dozens of languages, was written in the 1970s in Madrid: "You Have Come Down to the Lakeshore; *Tú has venido a la orilla*" (ELW 817). The song evokes a Galilee scene (Matthew 4), as translated by Madeleine Forell Marshall. Many know this melody (PESCADOR DE HOMBRES) and especially the personal refrain: "Sweet Lord, you have looked into my eyes." Marshall also translated another of Gabaráin's hymns now in various hymnals almost as often as "Pescador," namely, "Grains of Wheat; *Una espiga*" (*With One Voice* 708) as well as Alberto Taulé's Catalonian "All Earth is Hopeful; *Todo la tierra*" (ELW 266).[3]

Latin American songs have appeared in Lutheran and other hymnals from many sources, and especially through the work of Gerhard M. Cartford (1933–2016) at Texas Lutheran College in Sequin, Texas, and in Latin America. Born in Madagascar and educated in the United States with a Fulbright year in Norway, Cartford himself illustrates World Christianity, notably for his translations and arrangements of a dozen examples in *Evangelical Lutheran Worship*. From Central America came "The Lord Now Sends Us Forth; *Enviado soy de Dios*" (ELW 538). A Brazilian (Portuguese) folk song yielded a Spanish version and then "Oh, Sing to the Lord; *Cantad al Señor*" (ELW 822 and LSB 808). See also "Halle Halle Halleluja," a Caribbean melody arranged by Mark Sedio (ELW 172) and "When We Are Living; *Pues si vivimos*" (ELW 639). Pablo Sosa, a Methodist Argentinian, has composed, arranged, and translated

---

3   Gabaráin's U. S. distributor, Oregon Catholic Press, issued a statement in August 2021 that charges of child abuse against him have led them to remove his work from their website.

many hymns of international significance, and written some of his own: "Behold, How Pleasant; *Miren qué bueno*" (ELW 649) and "Heaven Is Singing for Joy; *El cielo canta alegría*" (ELW 664). Here too the list is expanding rapidly, including songs in Spanish or Portuguese from and for Pentecostal communities. Often the societal context is key, as in Rodolfo Gaede Neto's "For the Troubles and the Sufferings of the World; *Pelas dores deste mundo*" (ACS 1051) from Brazil.

East Asia

Before the Anti-Apartheid movement generated the South African songs that spread worldwide, and even before Vatican II encouraged the vernacular singing noted from Latin America, an East Asian hymn had already circulated widely as a preview of World Christianity. For an international and ecumenical Christian education convention in Tokyo in 1958, a Japanese Methodist pastor, Tokuo Yamaguchi (1900–95), wrote "Here, O Lord, Your Servants Gather; *Sekai no tomo to te o tsunagi*" (ELW 530) to match the convention's Johannine theme ("I am the way, and the truth, and the life," John 14:6). Yamaguchi's invocation of Jesus as savior, teacher, and healer was set to a traditional Japanese melody from the Gagaku Shinto court style by Isao Koizumi (1907–92). Although musically controversial in Japan, this hymn, as translated by Everett M. Stowe, quickly spread to hymnals around the world.[4]

As to the hymnody of World Christianity generally, perhaps the most important individual is also from the Pacific Rim, namely, Taiwan's I-to Loh (1936–). Son of a Presbyterian pastor and a musician mother, Loh's studies took him from the Tainan Theological College and Seminary to New York's Union Theological Seminary (School of Sacred Music) and then to the University of California Los Angeles for a 1982 PhD in ethnomusicology. Loh taught in the Philippines

---

4   Daniel T. Niles (1908–70) was also the translator, editor, and author of some East Asian hymns, such as ELW 748. Westermeyer's *ELW Companion* indicates, at 748 (p. 611), that Niles's corpus is less than once thought.

I-to Loh

(1982–94) and then back in Taiwan at the Tainan Seminary as Professor and President. He composed his own hymns, but also compiled dozens of collections of songs from all of East Asia in some early works and then especially in *Sound the Bamboo*, with 315 songs in 44 languages from 22 countries.[5] Loh also wrote overviews of these hymns: *Asian Hymns in their Cultural and Liturgical Contexts* (Chicago: GIA Publications, 2011) and *In Search of Asian Sounds and Symbols in Worship* (Singapore: Trinity Theological College, 2012). He and his work inspired many followers in East Asia and elsewhere. Most strikingly for our subject of World Christianity, Loh also translated, adapted, and/or arranged songs from India, Korea, Nigeria, Zimbabwe, and other parts of Africa. Christians around the globe owe much of their awareness of songs from other lands to I-to Loh.[6]

---

5   *Sound the Bamboo* (The Christian Conference of Asia Hymnal; Manilla, Philippines: Asian Institute for Liturgy and Music, 1990; Hong Kong: Christian Conference of Asia; Tainan, Taiwan: Taiwan Presbyterian Church Press, 2000).

6   See Swee Hong Lim, *Giving Voice to Asian Christians, An Appraisal of the Pioneering Work of I-to Loh in the Area of Congregational Song* (Saarbrücken, Germany: Verlag

There are some denominational-geographical patterns to note as well. Recent American hymnals among Presbyterians, for example, who are so numerous in South Korea, typically have dozens of hymns from those sources, such as Geonyong Lee's "Come Now, O Prince of Peace; *Ososŏ, ososŏ*" (ELW 247, also in *Glory to God* 103), also edited by I-to Loh. Illustrating that World Christianity means translations not only into English but also from English, some Presbyterian hymnals supply many Korean versions of hymns from other cultures. The traditional "Holy, Holy, Holy" (*Glory to God,* 1) is there presented in Heber's English as well as Spanish and Korean translations.

And More

Once a global horizon is in view, hymns from World Christianity can mean even more geographical diversity than glimpsed in these brief lines about Africa, Latin America, and East Asia.[7] Russian Orthodox liturgy (Kyrie, *With One Voice* 602) and Jamaican calypso ("Let Us Talent and Tongues Employ," ELW 674) come to mind, the latter written by Fred Kaan for the 1975 meeting of the World Council of Churches in Nairobi. The haunting fragment of a seventeenth-century Hungarian pastor's poem, paraphrased by Erik Routley from a prose translation, lives on as "There in God's Garden" (ELW 342).[8] Even closer to home for North Americans, yet from a non-European culture, is the Native American tune for "Many and Great, O God; *Wakantanka taku nitawa*" (ELW 837) first written in the Dakota language by Joseph R. Renville (1779–1846). The English paraphrase of stanzas 1 and 7 (originally the last) are by R. Philip Frazier. Renville set

---

Dr. Müller, 2008). Loh also edited *Seng-si* (2009), the hymnal of the Presbyterian Church in Taiwan.

7   For broader coverage, at least up until 2000, see the new chapter 32 in Routley-Richardson, *Panorama,* "World Hymnody (1976–2000)," pp. 633–672. From Europe also came Dietrich Bonhoeffer's "By Gracious Powers," ELW 626.

8   Routley cheerfully admitted to knowing not a word of Hungarian; Routley-Richardson, *Panorama,* p. 455.

Many and Great, O God, Are Your Works
Wakantanka taku nitawa

Text: Joseph R. Renville, 1779–1846; para. Philip Frazier, 1892–1964, alt.
Music: LAC QUI PARLE, Dakota tune; arr. *Songs of the People*, 1986
Arr. © 1986 Augsburg Publishing House, admin. Augsburg Fortress.

Duplication in any form prohibited without permission or valid license from copyright administrator.

it to the tune he called LAC QUI PARLE from the part of Minnesota that he and his Sioux mother (and I) called home. In a tragic turn, Dakota prisoners sang this hymn while led to their execution in 1862.[9]

Finally, there is another current form of Christian song that transcends national, cultural, and linguistic barriers without needing translation. As with vestiges of Hebrew (*Alleluia, Amen*) and Greek (*Kyrie*), the Latin tradition of the premodern church, kept alive in *Gloria in excelsis Deo* and *Dona nobis pacem,* has made a comeback along with monastic or Gregorian chant. The ecumenical Taizé community in France, where Benedictine monasticism had major medieval revivals, has sparked a renewal of monastic chant and Latin phrases now sung around the world. The simple *Veni, Sancte Spiritus* ("Holy Spirit, Come to Us," ELW 406) is sung in harmonic repetition in many contexts, thanks to Jacques Berthier (1923–94). The text echoes a medieval refrain from Pentecost, the biblical event that itself transcended linguistic barriers. Many of Berthier's Taizé songs are in English, now also a global language, but the spirit of the movement comes from the Latin plainsong, as seen in *Ubi caritas et amor, Deus ibi est,* a ninth-century text. ELW 642 and 653 translate it as "Where True Charity and Love Abide"; see also ELW 359. Berthier set many biblical phrases to simple chants, such as "Jesus, Remember Me" (Luke 23:42, ELW 616), "O Lord, Hear My Prayer" (Psalm 102:1–2, ELW 751), and others not needing hymnals at all.[10]

The venerable Celtic monastery of Iona, on a small island off the coast of Scotland, has also been invoked by a modern Iona Community with its commitments to peace and justice expressed in music. Scottish Presbyterian John Bell (1949–) writes texts and adapts melodies in this folk-song vein, such as "Will You Come and Follow Me" (ELW 798) and "Take, Oh, Take Me as I Am" (ELW 814). Bell has also

---

9   See details under author Joseph Renville at www.Hymnary.org (accessed Dec. 29, 2022).

10   See also ELW 175, 236, 262, 348, 388, 472 (with credit to Robert Batastini), and 528.

arranged some of the African "freedom songs" covered earlier (ELW 253, 721, 741; see also *All Creation Sings* 972, 978).

In translations and otherwise, the hymns of World Christianity can transcend linguistic, confessional, and national borders. They are ecumenical and yet retain indigenous cultures and traditions, a hallmark of current Christian history.

Postscript

The singing church has a long history, as only glimpsed in the pages of this book. The Taizé hymns have brought us full circle. They are sung Scripture, where this narrative began, as are so many of the hymns of the singing church through the ages. Further, many are in Latin, the language of the ancient Roman Empire and much of western church history. Biblical Hebrew and Greek are also still sung, at Taizé and in churches of all kinds worldwide. Simple words sung from ancient languages frame our worship: *Kyrie eleison,* Lord, have mercy, names our need; *Alleluia* is our praise and thanks to God; *Amen,* it is true, gets the last word. Israel's singing became the New Testament's hymnody, and for centuries the church has sung on.

Hearing the music is not enough. Communal Christian formation comes from singing the words together. The texts of the singing church bridge not only the ages but also many confessional differences today. Singing church history has long granted the faithful blessings unawares; knowing more about these hymn texts can multiply and spread such gifts.

POSTLUDE

HYMN TEXTS CAN guide us not only through church history but also through the church year, as well as into basic Christian doctrine and ecumenical awareness. Materials from this book could be used for various topics, once put in a different order.

Hymns for the Church Year

Certain hymn texts presented above in their original contexts and thus in historical sequence could also accompany and enrich the liturgical seasons from Advent through Pentecost. The main suggestions here are followed in each season by other options, with some ideas for the Sundays after Pentecost as well.

Advent: "Savior of the Nations, Come," St. Ambrose, fourth century, ELW 263, LSB 332. "Wake, Awake," P. Nicolai, 1599, ELW 436, LSB 516. "All Earth Is Hopeful; *Toda la tierra,*" Alberto Taulé, World Christianity, ELW 266. "Come Now, O Prince of Peace; *Ososǒ, ososǒ,*" Geonyong Lee, World Christianity, ELW 247.

Christmas: "Of the Father's Love Begotten," Prudentius, fifth century, ELW 295, LSB 384. "Lo, How a Rose E'er Blooming," late medieval, ELW 272, LSB 359.

Epiphany: "The Only Son from Heaven," Elisabeth Cruciger, sixteenth century, ELW 309, LSB 402. "Hail Thee, Festival Day," Fortunatus, sixth century, ELW 394, LSB 489.

Lent: "Jesus, the Very Thought of You" and "O Jesus, Joy of Loving Hearts," attr. Bernard of Clairvaux, twelfth century, ELW 754 and ELW 658, LSB 554. "Oh, Love, How Deep, How Broad, How High," attr. Thomas à Kempis, fifteenth century, ELW 322, LSB 544. "There in God's Garden," tr. Erik Routley, World Christianity, ELW 342.

Palm Sunday: "All Glory, Laud, and Honor," Theodulph of Orléans, ninth century, ELW 344, LSB 442.

Good Friday: "O Sacred Head, Now Wounded," attr. Bernard of Clairvaux, twelfth century, ELW 351–52, LSB 449–50. "Jesus, Remember Me," Taizé, World Christianity, ELW 616.

Easter: "Come, You Faithful" and "The Day of Resurrection," John of Damascus, eighth century, ELW 363 and 361, LSB 487 and 478. "Christ Jesus Lay in Death's Strong Bands," Martin Luther, sixteenth century, ELW 370, LSB 458, and related prior hymns. "Christ Has Arisen, Alleluia; *Mfurahini, haleluya*," Bernard Kyamanywa, World Christianity, ELW 364 and LSB 466.

Pentecost: "Creator Spirit," Rhabanus Maurus, ninth century, ELW 577–78, LSB 498–99. "Come Holy Ghost, God and Lord," Martin Luther, sixteenth century, ELW 395, LSB 497. "Gracious Spirit, Heed Our Pleading; *Njoo kwetu, Roho mwema*," Wilson Niwagila, World Christianity, ELW 401.

Trinity: "All Glory Be to God on High," Nikolaus Decius, sixteenth century, ELW 410, LSB 947. "We All Believe in One True God," Martin Luther, sixteenth century, ELW 411, LSB 953–54.

Ordinary Time, Sundays after Pentecost, thematic and chronological order:

General: the *Te Deum*, early medieval, ELW 228, LSB 223–25.
Creation: "All Creatures, Worship God Most High," St. Francis, thirteenth century, ELW 835. "Many and Great, O God; *Wakantanka taku nitawa*," Joseph R. Renville, World Christianity, ELW 837.
Justification: "Dear Christians, One and All, Rejoice," Martin Luther, sixteenth century, ELW 594, LSB 556. "That Priceless Grace," Emmanuel F. Y. Grantson, World Christianity, ELW 591.
Sanctification: "Love Divine, All Loves Excelling," Charles Wesley, eighteenth century, ELW 631, LSB 700.

Racial Justice: "Lift Every Voice and Sing," Johnson brothers, ca. 1900, ELW 841, LSB 964.

Social Causes: "God of Grace and God of Glory," Harry Emerson Fosdick, mid-twentieth century, ELW 705, LSB 850. "Jesu, Jesu, Fill Us with Your Love," Tom Colvin, World Christianity, ELW 708 and LSB 980. "For the Troubles and the Sufferings of the World; *Pelas dores deste mundo*" Rodolfo Gaede Neto, World Christianity, *All Creation Sings*, 1051.

Global Awareness: "We Are Marching in the Light; *Siyahamba*," South African, World Christianity, ELW 866.

Hymns for Catechetical/Doctrinal Overview

For Lutheran catechesis, Martin Luther's own hymn settings have long been attached to the various sections of his *Small Catechism.* These hymns could survey Christian teaching all by themselves, although some are less familiar than others. For a wider range of hymn writers and of specific topics, the list below is merely a suggested starting point. For a much larger array, see Philip H. Pfatteicher, *The People's Theology: Classic Hymns and Christian Formation* (Chicago: GIA Publications, 2020).

Martin Luther's Catechetical Hymns

Perhaps most of Luther's hymns could be considered catechetical, but the 1543 Wittenberg hymnal paired specific hymns with sections of the catechism, as mentioned above in the chapter on Luther. Robin Leaver has presented these hymns, plus an introductory hymn and a concluding one, in his excellent book *Luther's Liturgical Music,* under the heading of "Musical Catechesis." Robin A. Leaver, *Luther's Liturgical Music: Principles and Implications* (Grand Rapids, MI: Eerdmans, 2007), 107–69.

Introduction. "Lord, Keep Us Steadfast in Your Word," ELW 517, LSB 655, LW 53: 304–305.

The Ten Commandments. "These are the Holy Ten Commands," LSB 581, LW 53: 277–79. See also the shorter "Man, Wouldst Thou Live All Blissfully?," LW 53: 280–281.

The Creed. "We All Believe in One True God," ELW 411, LSB 953–53, LW 53: 271–273.

The Lord's Prayer. "Our Father, God in Heaven Above," ELW 746–77, LSB 766, LW 53: 295–298.

Baptism. "To Jordan Came the Christ, Our Lord," LSB 406, LBW 79, LW 53: 299–301.

Repentance. "Out of the Depths I Cry to You," ELW 600, LSB 607, LW 53: 221–224.

The Lord's Supper. "Jesus Christ, Our Blessed Savior," LSB 627, LW 53: 249–251; *All Creation Sings*, 963.

Conclusion. "Dear Christians, One and All, Rejoice," ELW 594, LSB 556, LW 53: 217–220.

Various Other Hymns for Doctrinal Overview

God/Trinity. Besides hymnic versions of the Creed, "We Praise You, O God" (the *Te Deum*), early medieval, ELW 228, LSB 223–25, 939–41. "All Glory Be to God on High," Nikolaus Decius, sixteenth century, ELW 310, LSB 947.

Creation. "All Creatures, Worship God Most High," St. Francis, thirteenth century, ELW 835. "Many and Great, O God; *Wakantanka taku nitawa*," Joseph R. Renville, World Christianity, ELW 837.

Law/Repentance. See the Luther hymns mentioned, "These are the Holy Ten Commands" (LSB 581) and "Out of the Depths I Cry to You" (ELW 600, LSB 607).

Incarnation, Birth, and Epiphany. Advent: "Savior of the Nations, Come," St. Ambrose, fourth century, ELW 263,

LSB 332; "All Earth Is Hopeful; *Toda la tierra*," Alberto Taulé, World Christianity, ELW 266. Christmas: "Of the Father's Love Begotten," Prudentius, fifth century, ELW 295, LSB 384. Epiphany: "The Only Son from Heaven," Elisabeth Cruciger, sixteenth century, ELW 309, LSB 402.

Incarnation, Suffering, and Death. "Oh, Love, How Deep, How Broad, How High," attr. Thomas à Kempis, fifteenth century, ELW 322, LSB 544. "There in God's Garden," tr. Erik Routley, World Christianity, ELW 342. "O Sacred Head, Now Wounded," attr. Bernard of Clairvaux, twelfth century, ELW 351, LSB 449–450.

Resurrection. "The Day of Resurrection!" and "Come, You Faithful, Raise the Strain," John of Damascus, eighth century, ELW 361 and LSB 478, ELW 363 and LSB 487. "Christ Jesus Lay in Death's Strong Bands," Martin Luther, sixteenth century, ELW 370, LSB 458. "Christ Has Arisen, Alleluia; *Mfurahini, haleluya*," Bernard Kyamanywa, World Christianity, ELW 364 and LSB 466.

Holy Spirit. "Creator Spirit, Heavenly Dove" and "Come, Holy Ghost, Creator Blest," Attr. Rhabanus Maurus, ninth century, ELW 577–78 and LSB 498–499. "Gracious Spirit, Heed Our Pleading; *Njoo kwetu, Roho mwema*," Wilson Niwagila, World Christianity, ELW 401.

Justification. "Dear Christians, One and All, Rejoice," Martin Luther, sixteenth century, ELW 594, LSB 556. "That Priceless Grace," Emmanuel F. Y. Grantson, World Christianity, ELW 591.

Sanctification. "Love Divine, All Loves Excelling," Charles Wesley, eighteenth century, ELW 631, LSB 700.

[For repentance, baptism, Lord's Supper, see Luther's catechetical hymns above.]

Lord's Supper, general. "Grains of Wheat; *Una espiga*," Cesáreo Gabaráin, World Christianity, *With One Voice* 708.

Lord's Supper, Divine Liturgy (Orthodox). "Let All Mortal Flesh Keep Silence," Greek liturgy, fifth century, ELW 490, LSB 621.

Lord's Supper, the Mass (Roman Catholic). "Thee We Adore," Thomas Aquinas, thirteenth century, ELW 476, LSB 640.

Justice, Peace. "God of Grace and God of Glory," Harry Emerson Fosdick, twentieth century, ELW 706, LSB 850. "Jesu, Jesu, Fill Us with Your Love," Tom Colvin, World Christianity, ELW 708 and LSB 980. "For the Troubles and the Sufferings of the World; *Pelas dores deste mundo*" Rodolfo Gaede Neto, World Christianity, *All Creation Sings* 1051.

Discipleship, Vocation. "You Have Come Down to the Lakeshore; *Tú has venido a la orilla*, Cesáreo Gabaráin, World Christianity, ELW 817. "The Lord Now Sends Us Forth," World Christianity, ELW 538.

Witness. "Oh, for a Thousand Tongues to Sing," Charles Wesley, eighteenth century, ELW 886. "Let Us Talents and Tongues Employ," Fred Kaan, World Christianity, ELW 674.

Hymns for Ecumenical Awareness

Hymn texts can also increase our ecumenical awareness of other Christian communities. It is interesting to note which hymns by Martin Luther or other distinctively Lutheran hymns are included in various denominational hymnals. For example, a Roman Catholic hymnal such as *Choral Praise,* 3rd ed. (Portland, OR: OCP, 2012), approved by the US Conference of Bishops, has Catholics singing Luther's "Mighty Fortress" and Martin Rinckhart's "Now Thank We All Our God," plus Watts, C. Wesley, Thomas Dorsey, and spirituals galore. The chronological presentations in this book have touched on representative hymns from several denominations, often with distinctive doctrinal emphases.

An Eastern Orthodox emphasis on Christ as the meeting point of the human and the divine, in the incarnation and in the resurrection, is represented by John of Damascus, especially in his Easter hymns "The Day of Resurrection!" (ELW 361, LSB 478) and "Come, You Faithful, Raise the Strain" (ELW 363, LSB 487). See chapter three above.

The distinctive Roman Catholic doctrine of transubstantiation regarding Christ's presence in the bread and wine is apparent in "Thee, We Adore" (ELW 476, LSB 640). See the section on Thomas Aquinas in chapter five.

The Reformed tradition (Presbyterians, for example) is naturally part of chapter seven on the Reformation, at least in the brief conclusion about the Geneva Psalter. The stress in some Reformed circles historically on singing only scriptural words, especially the Psalms, is also mentioned in chapter nine. The obvious example would be Psalm 100 in "All People That on Earth Do Dwell" (ELW 883, LSB 791).

The Moravian Brethren emphasis on Christ's suffering and specific wounds was mentioned in chapter eight on Pietists and in chapter nine on John Wesley's translation of von Zinzendorf's "Jesus, Your Blood and Righteousness" (LBW 302, LSB 563).

The Methodists have always stressed holiness, as presented in chapter nine. This emphasis on sanctification and some early disputes about it are glimpsed in Charles Wesley's "Love Divine, All Loves Excelling" (ELW 631, LSB 700).

For background to American Evangelicals, see Fanny Crosby's "Blessed Assurance" (ELW 638) in chapter ten. Several related hymns and hymn writers in that chapter are good representatives of the non-denominational revivals of the nineteenth century.

African American churches (chapter eleven) of many different denominations sing "Lift Every Voice and Sing" (ELW 841, LSB 964) and identify with it, as well as Thomas A. Dorsey's more individual "Precious Lord" (ELW 73, LSB 739).

Finally, the World Christianity phenomenon in chapter twelve is well represented by "Siyahamba" (ELW 866). Just as it crossed linguistic lines, from South Africa's Zulu/Xhosa to Swedish and then to English and other languages, so it and other examples of global hymns cross many denominational distinctions in the ecumenical church today.

APPENDIX

Discussion Questions

Appended discussion prompts for classes or reading groups; reflection prompts for individuals.

For every chapter:

1. Pick one hymn to read aloud, perhaps one stanza by each willing participant, pausing between stanzas to share responses or impressions from hearing it together. If the tune is familiar, sing a stanza or two, with or without accompaniment.
2. For familiar hymns, what new information or insights did you gain?
3. For unfamiliar hymns, what was most surprising or intriguing to you, and why?

One. Prelude; Psalms, Canticles, and Other Biblical Refrains

1. Consider the idea of making Christian paraphrases of Old Testament texts, for example, understanding the "Lord is my shepherd" as Christ, or the bride and groom in the Song of Songs as the church/soul and Christ. What are some good reasons for and against this pattern?
2. Which familiar hymns surprised you for being based on Scripture? "Joy to the World"? "Jesus Shall Reign"?
3. Look up and discuss the biblical sources for these liturgical texts:

Kyrie (Matthew 15:22, 17:15, 20:30)
Gloria (Luke 2)
Sanctus (Isaiah 6 and Revelation 4)
Benedictus (Matthew 21:9)
Agnus Dei (John 1)

4. What do *Alleluia* and *Amen* mean, from Hebrew, and *Kyrie Eleison*, from Greek? What do *Gloria, Sanctus, Benedictus,* and *Agnus Dei* mean, from Latin? What do you think about singing words from languages other than your own, whether ancient or modern?

Two. The Early Church, Western and Latin (100–500)

1. Read the Nicene Creed, especially the Second Article about Christ, and compare it to the language in the hymns by Ambrose and/or Prudentius.
2. Look closely at the wording of the *Gloria Patri*, specifically the prepositions, as opposing an (Arian) subordination of the Son, namely, equally "to" the Father and "to" the Son and "to" the Holy Spirit, not "through" the Son and "in" the Holy Spirit. Further, compare "as it was in the beginning" with Arius: "there was, when he (Christ) was not."
3. As to the big change from the lack of evidence for hymns in the second and third century to the abundance of sung texts in the fourth century, was the public favor and money from Emperor Constantine and his successors a good thing or a bad thing?
4. As to the legendary St. Patrick and "I Bind unto Myself Today," how would you assess binding ourselves to the natural world? How about to the angelic world?

Three. The Eastern and Orthodox Early Church (100–800)

1. For you, is "Let All Mortal Flesh Keep Silence" a communion hymn? Read the pertinent stanzas aloud.
2. Consider what it means to believe, with John of Damascus
   and Eastern Orthodoxy in general, that the incarnation is
   the union of the human and the divine and that therefore all
   humanity is in Christ reunited to God and included in the
   resurrection.
3. In "Come, You Faithful" what are the parallels between the
   Exodus and the resurrection? What does that pattern imply
   about Christian appreciation for the Old Testament?
4. Listen to some recordings of Orthodox chant, whether in
   English (the Orthodox Church in America) or perhaps the
   Syrian type that spread to Iraq/Iran and to Ethiopia.
5. Find Kassia's full text and consider anew the story and significance of Mary Magdalene.

Four. The "Dark" Ages? The Early Middle Ages (500–1100)

1. Which hymn text for you best refutes the image of the "dark"
   (uneducated/unenlightened) Middle Ages?
2. Look closely at the full text of the *Te Deum*. What are the
   biblical and liturgical elements? How would you assess its
   theological challenges?
3. In "Creator Spirit" by Rhabanus Maurus, what all does the
   Holy Spirit do?
4. What difference is made to the Nicene Creed by adding the
   filioque ("and the Son")? Does saying that the Holy Spirit is
   "of both" the Father and the Son mean support in "Creator
   Spirit" for the *filioque*?

5. What would it be like to sing, as the Benedictines did, all 150 Psalms as a community every week for the rest of your life?

Five. Saints Bernard, Francis, and Thomas Aquinas; The High Middle Ages (1100–1300)

1. For you, which of these hymn writers has the most interesting or memorable life story and why?
2. How do you evaluate the traditional understanding of the bride and groom in the Song of Songs as representing the soul and Christ?
3. For "O Sacred Head," what do you make of all the dropped stanzas? Is the bloody image disturbing to you?
4. For Francis, how do you evaluate addressing the sun and moon as if they were living beings (or divine) instead of addressing only God as the creator?
5. For Thomas Aquinas and his sacramental piety, what does "transubstantiation" mean? How might you apply his hymn to your own understanding of Holy Communion?

Six. Reforms before the Reformation: The Late Middle Ages (1300–1500)

1. Have you ever sung or heard the *Dies Irae* or the *Stabat Mater*? If so, was it at a worship service or a concert? How would you describe your experience?
2. Which "reform" before the Reformation is to you the most surprising or significant?
3. Which of the vernacular (English, German) carols was surprising to you as to having medieval origins?
4. What parts of "Oh, Love, How Deep" strike you as anticipating the Protestant Reformation?

5. How might we evaluate the Hussite "heresy," and what do you make of Luther's admission that "we are all Hussites without knowing it"?

Seven. Martin Luther and the Reformation (1500–1600)

1. What is your favorite "Luther hymn," and why?
2. Which hymn by Luther surprised you for being biblical or liturgical or "medieval" as to textual source?
3. Read "Dear Christians, One and All" aloud as Luther's own testimony or a sermonic proclamation. How might you apply it to your own experience?
4. Read aloud Elisabeth Cruciger's hymn, noting especially the stanzas that are often dropped, and consider how she was (almost) erased from memory.
5. How might we evaluate the Reformed tradition's emphasis on the Psalms and its insistence on using only close translations of them rather than loose paraphrases?

Eight. Lutherans and Pietists (1600–1750)

1. As Protestants split and diversified, what does "Pietism" mean to you and how does it cross denominational borders?
2. For Philipp Nicolai, how did the plague in his time affect his hymn texts? How might we apply his texts to health crises today, whether individual or societal or global?
3. How do you assess the emphasis on the language of bride and bridegroom in "Wake, Awake" and its absence in translations of "O Morning Star"?
4. For a musical treat, listen to part or all of J. S. Bach's Cantata 140, *Wachet auf*, following along with an English translation.

Nine. Isaac Watts and the Wesley Brothers (1700–1800)

1. How might we evaluate Watts's Christian appropriation of the Psalms, as in "The Lord [Jesus] is my shepherd"?
2. Which "Wesley" hymns do you know and like best, and why?
3. How were John and Charles Wesley bridges from Europe to the New World, especially in their hymnody?
4. In "Love Divine, All Loves Excelling," consider how aspects of sanctification are subtly suggested. Is sanctification sudden or gradual? Is it complete now or only in the future?

Ten. American Revivals and the Social Gospel (1800–1950)

1. Consider how blindness might have shaped Fanny Crosby's capacity for memory and her patterns of songwriting.
2. How does "Blessed Assurance" have roots in a Wesleyan holiness and assurance of salvation?
3. For Walter Rauschenbusch and Harry Fosdick, personal renewal and social renewal went together; assess how spirituality and social action today often seem like two different topics.
4. How might we articulate the difference between "nondenominational" and "ecumenical" today?

Eleven. African American Hymnody (1800–)

1. How might we think of "Lift Every Voice and Sing" as an anthem *and* as a hymn?
2. Ponder whether everyone should sing "Lift Every Voice," or only those whose families have experienced what it expresses.
3. How do we evaluate bringing into church the "world's" music, whether blues, jazz, pop, or rap?
4. How is Thomas Dorsey's personal experience shared by others?

Twelve. World Christianity (1950–)

1. Which of these recent hymns was already familiar to you, and what do you think of singing it or others in another language?
2. How might we evaluate the ecumenical effect of shared hymnody, with a common Christian core but diverse musical forms and languages?
3. Which of these hymns have previously or now introduced you to other cultures?
4. Share any experience you have had with the Taizé materials, and/or singing in Latin.

Postlude

A. Hymns for the Church Year: do the liturgical seasons (like Advent and Christmas; or Lent, Holy Week, and Easter) stay separate for you or blend together?
B. Hymns for Catechetical/Doctrinal Overview: which hymns seem more like "sermons in song" and which are more like prayers?
C. Hymns for Ecumenical Awareness: insofar as you have experienced worship services in other denominations, what was different about their singing and what was familiar? Consider specific hymns, types of music, forms of leadership and accompaniment, congregational level of participation.

Overall, in conclusion:

What were the biggest surprises for you in this hymn history?

Consider compiling your own "hymn history," namely, a timeline of favorite and important hymns in your life, from earliest memories through adolescence into adulthood, perhaps marking some of life's milestones up to today.

What do you want people to sing at your funeral?

ABBREVIATIONS

BIBLICAL BOOKS ARE abbreviated according to the New Revised Standard Version. Hymnals and other publications listed here have full entries in the bibliography.

ACS	= *All Creation Sings*
attr.	= attributed to
ca.	= circa, around
CE	= Common Era
ELW	= *Evangelical Lutheran Worship*
ELW Companion	= Paul Westermeyer, *Hymnal Companion to Evangelical Lutheran Worship*
Hymns and Hymnody	= *Hymns and Hymnody, Historical and Theological Introductions*
LBW	= *Lutheran Book of Worship*
LSB	= *Lutheran Service Book*
LSB Companion	= *Lutheran Service Book Companion to the Hymns*
LW	= *Luther's Works*
RB	= Rule of St. Benedict
Routley-Richardson, *Panorama*	= Erik Routley, *A Panorama of Christian Hymnody*
SBH	= *Service Book and Hymnal*
st. and sts.	= stanza and stanzas
WOV	= *With One Voice*

BIBLIOGRAPHY, WITH HYMNALS

Armstrong, R. and I. Brady, trans. *Francis and Clare, the Complete Works*. New York: Paulist Press, 1982.

Belcher, Kimberly. "Trinitarian Hymns in the East and West." In *From Asia Minor to Western Europe*, edited by Mark A. Lamport, Benjamin K. Forrest, and Vernon M. Whaley, 95–105. Vol. 1 of *Hymns and Hymnody*. Eugene, OR: Cascade Books, 2019.

Benedict, Bruce H. and Lester Ruth. "Retuned Hymn Movement." In *From the English West to the Global South*, edited by Mark A. Lamport, Benjamin K. Forrest, and Vernon M. Whaley, 301–314. Vol. 3 of *Hymns and Hymnody*. Eugene, OR: Cascade Books, 2019.

Berger, Teresa. *Theology in Hymns*. Nashville: Abingdon, 1985.

Blumhofer, Edith. *Her Heart Can See: The Life and Hymns of Fanny J. Crosby*. Grand Rapids, MI: Eerdmans, 2005.

Booker, Vaughn A. *Lift Every Voice and Swing: Black Musicians and Religious Culture in the Jazz Century*. New York: New York University Press, 2020.

Bradshaw, Paul. *Two Ways of Prayer*. Nashville: Abingdon, 1995.

Brita, Antonella. "Yared." In *Encyclopaedia Aethiopica*, edited by Alessandro Bausi, 26–28. Vol. 5. Wiesbaden: Harrossowitz, 2014.

Brown, C. Boyd. *Singing the Gospel: Lutheran Hymns and the Success of the Reformation*. Cambridge, MA: Harvard University Press, 2005.

Buszin, Walter. "Walter, Johann." In *The Encyclopedia of the Lutheran Church*, edited by J. Bodensieck, 2452–2454. Minneapolis: Augsburg Publishing House, 1965.

Christman, Robert. "The Antwerp Martyrs and Luther's First Song," *Lutheran Quarterly* 36 (2022): 373–389.

Chrysostomides, Anna. "John of Damascus' Theology of Icons in the Context of Eighth-Century Palestinian Iconoclasm," *Dumbarton Oaks Papers* 75 (2021): 263–295.

Coakley, John W. and Andrea Sterk, eds. *Readings in World Christian History,* vol. 1, *Earliest Christianity to 1453.* Maryknoll, New York: Orbis Books, 2004.

Cone, Cecil Wayne. *The Identity Crisis in Black Theology.* Nashville: AME Church, 1975.

Cone, James H. *Said I Wasn't Gonna Tell Nobody.* Maryknoll, New York: Orbis Books, 2018.

Dunkle, Brian P., SJ. *Enchantment and Creed in the Hymns of Ambrose of Milan.* Oxford: Oxford University Press, 2016.

Evans, Christopher H. *The Kingdom Is Always but Coming: A Life of Walter Rauschenbusch.* Grand Rapids, MI: Eerdmans, 2004.

Faithful, George. "A More Brotherly Song, a Less Passionate Passion," *Church History* 82.4 (2013): 779–811.

Firth, Catherine. See Loewe, Andreas.

Fosdick, Harry E. *The Living of these Days: An Autobiography.* New York: Harper & Row, 1956.

Froehlich, Karlfried. "Discerning the Voices: Praise and Lament in the Tradition of the Christian Psalter," *Calvin Theological Journal* 36 (2001): 75–90.

Gordley, Matthew E. *New Testament Christological Hymns.* Downers Grove, IL: IVP Academic, 2018.

———. *Teaching through Song in Antiquity.* Tübingen: Mohr Siebeck, 2011.

Grafton, Anthony. "Middle Ages," *The Dictionary of the Middle Ages,* Vol. 8, 308–309. New York: Charles Scribner's Sons, 1987.

Grindal, Gracia. *Preaching from Home: The Stories of Seven Lutheran Women Hymn Writers.* Grand Rapids, MI: Eerdmans, 2001.

Haemig, Mary Jane. "Elisabeth Cruciger (1500? –1535): The Case of the Disappearing Hymn Writer," *Sixteenth Century Journal* 32 (2001): 21–44.

———. "Elisabeth Cruciger (ca 1500–1535)." In *Women Reformers of Early Modern Europe,* edited by Kirsi Stjerna, 34–42. Minneapolis: Fortress Press, 2022.

Hamm, Berndt. *The Early Luther: Stages in a Reformation Reorientation.* Grand Rapids, MI: Eerdmans, 2014.

Harris, Michael W. *The Rise of Gospel Blues: The Music of Thomas Andrew Dorsey in the Urban Church.* New York: Oxford University Press, 1992.

Herl, Joseph. "Germany from 1620 to the Present." In *Lutheran Service Book Companion to the Hymns,* vol. 2, 27–50. St. Louis: Concordia, 2019.

Herl, Joseph, Peter C. Reske, and Jon D. Vieker, eds. *Lutheran Service Book Companion to the Hymns.* 2 volumes. St. Louis: Concordia, 2019.

Holeton, David and Hana Vlhorá-Wörner. "The Second Life of Jan Hus: Liturgy, Commemoration, Music." In *A Companion to Jan Hus,* edited by F. Šmohel, 289–324. Leiden: Brill, 2015.

Hymns and Hymnody. Historical and Theological Introductions. Volume 1: *From Asia Minor to Western Europe;* Volume 2: *From Catholic Europe to Protestant Europe;* Volume 3: *From the English West to the Global South.* Edited by Mark A. Lamport, Benjamin K. Forrest, and Vernon M. Whaley. Eugene, OR: Cascade Books, 2019.

Jarjour, Tala. "Syriac Song in the Early Centuries." In *From Asia Minor to Western Europe,* edited by Mark A. Lamport, Benjamin K. Forrest, and Vernon M. Whaley, 36–48. Vol. 1 of *Hymns and Hymnody.* Eugene, OR: Cascade Books, 2019.

Kerr, Hugh. *Readings in Christian Thought,* 2nd ed. Nashville: Abingdon, 1990.

Kolb, Robert and Timothy Wengert, eds. *The Book of Concord.* Minneapolis: Fortress Press, 2000.

Kolodziej, Benjamin. "Early Lutheran Hymnody (1550–1650)." In *From Catholic Europe to Protestant Europe,* edited by Mark A. Lamport, Benjamin K. Forrest, and Vernon M. Whaley, 31–48. Vol. 2 of *Hymns and Hymnody.* Eugene, OR: Cascade Books, 2019.

Krispin, Gerald. "Paul Gerhardt (1670–76), A Theologian Sifted in Satan's Sieve." In *Lives and Writings of the Great Fathers of the Lutheran Church,* edited by Timothy Schmeling, 229–242. St. Louis: Concordia, 2016.

Leaver, Robin. "*Psalms and Hymns* and *Hymns and Sacred Poems:* Two Strands of Wesleyan Hymn Collections." In *Music and The Wesleys,* edited by Nicholas Temperley and Stephen Banfield, 41–51. Chicago: University of Chicago Press, 2010.

———, ed. *A New Song We Now Begin: Celebrating the Half Millennium of Lutheran Hymnals 1524–2024.* Minneapolis, MN: Fortress Press, 2024.

————, ed. *Luther's Liturgical Music.* Grand Rapids, MI: Eerdmans, 2007.

————, ed. *The Whole Church Sings.* Grand Rapids, MI: Eerdmans, 2017.

Lim, Swee Hong. *Giving Voice to Asian Christians, An Appraisal of the Pioneering Work of I-to Loh in the Area of Congregational Song.* Saarbrücken, Germany: Verlag Dr. Müller, 2008.

Loewe, Andreas and Katherine Firth. "Martin Luther's 'Mighty Fortress.'" *Lutheran Quarterly* 32 (2018): 125–145.

Louth, Andrew. *St. John Damascene, Tradition and Originality in Byzantine Theology.* Oxford: Oxford University Press, 2002.

Luther, Martin. *Luther's Works,* American Edition, edited by Jaroslav Pelikan and Helmut T. Lehmann, volumes 1–55; Christopher Boyd Brown, volumes 56–80. St. Louis and Philadelphia: Concordia and Fortress, 1955—

Mann, Robert C. *The Church Sings Its Faith.* Chicago: GIA Publications, 2022.

Marisson, Michael and Daniel R. Melamed. www.bachcantatatexts.org.

McGinn, Bernard. *The Flowering of Mysticism. Men and Women in the New Mysticism 1200–1350.* Vol. 3 of *The Presence of God. A History of Western Christian Mysticism.* New York: Crossroad, 1998.

McVey, Kathleen E., trans. *Ephrem the Syrian: Hymns.* With an introduction by Kathleen E. McVey. New York: Paulist Press, 1989.

Meyendorff, John. "Filioque." In *The Dictionary of the Middle Ages,* vol. 5, 62–63. New York: Charles Scribner's Sons, 1987.

Miller, Robert M. *Harry Emerson Fosdick: Preacher, Pastor, Prophet.* New York: Oxford University Press, 1985.

Mumme, Jonathan. "Philipp Nicolai (1556–1608): Mystic-Orthodox Polemicist," *Lives and Writings of the Great Fathers of the Lutheran Church,* edited by Timothy Schmeling, 37–54. St. Louis: Concordia, 2016.

Neale, John Mason. "English Hymnody: Its History and Prospects," *Christian Remembrance* 18 (1850): 302–343, cited in *Hymns and Hymnody,* vol. 1, 170–171.

Nicolai, Philipp. *The Joy of Eternal Life,* translated by Matthew Carver. St. Louis: Concordia, 2021.

Noll, Mark A. *Turning Points: Decisive Moments in the History of Christianity.* Grand Rapids, MI: Baker, 1997.

Nuelsen, John. *John Wesley and the German Hymn.* Calverley: A. S. Holbrook, 1972.

O'Daly, Gerard. *Days Linked by Song; Prudentius' Cathemerinon.* Oxford: Oxford University Press, 2012.

Perry, Imani. *May We Forever Stand: A History of the Black National Anthem.* Chapel Hill, NC: The University of North Carolina Press, 2018.

Pfatteicher, Philip A. *The People's Theology: Classic Hymns and Christian Formation.* Chicago: GIA Publications, 2020.

Pitts, Wm. Lee. *The Reception of Rauschenbusch.* Macon, GA: Mercer University Press, 2018.

Rauschenbusch, Walter. *A Rauschenbusch Reader: The Kingdom of God and the Social Gospel,* compiled by Benson Y. Landis. New York: Harper, 1957.

Riley-Smith, Jonathan. "Crusading as an Act of Love." *History* 65 (1980): 177–192.

Robert, Michael. *The Humblest Sparrow: The Poetry of Venantius Fortunatus.* Ann Arbor, MI: University of Michigan Press, 2009.

Rorem, Paul. "The Company of Medieval Women Theologians." *Theology Today* 60.1 (2003): 82–93.

Routley, Erik. *A Panorama of Christian Hymnody,* edited and expanded by Paul A. Richardson. Chicago: GIA Publications, 2005; first edition, Collegeville, MN: Liturgical Press, 1979.

Ruff, Anthony. "The Early Church and the Middle Ages." In *Lutheran Service Book Companion,* vol. 2, edited by Joseph Herl, Peter C. Reske, and Jon D. Vieker, 3–12. St. Louis: Concordia, 2019.

Ruth, Lester. See Benedict, Bruce H.

Samra, Jim. "Hymns and Creedal Worship in the New Testament." In *From Asia Minor to Western Europe,* edited by Mark A. Lamport, Benjamin K. Forrest, and Vernon M. Whaley, 3–15. Vol. 1 of *Hymns and Hymnody.* Eugene, OR: Cascade Books, 2019.

Schwarz, Hans. "Trust in God in Trying Times: The Hymns of Paul Gerhardt," *Word and World* 43.2 (Spring 2023): 175–183.

Sherry, Kurt. *Kassia the Nun in Context: The Religious Thought of a Ninth-Century Byzantine Monastic.* Piscataway, NJ: Gorgias Press, 2013.

Simut, Cornelius C. "John Calvin and the Complete French Psalter." In *From Catholic Europe to Protestant Europe,* edited by Mark A.

Lamport, Benjamin K. Forrest, and Vernon M. Whaley, 49–63. Vol. 2 of *Hymns and Hymnody*. Eugene, OR: Cascade Books, 2019.

Skrekas, Dimitrios. "Byzantine Song in the Early Centuries, From Kantakion to the Canon." In *From Asia Minor to Western Europe*, edited by Mark A. Lamport, Benjamin K. Forrest, and Vernon M. Whaley, 64–80. Vol. 1 of *Hymns and Hymnody*. Eugene, OR: Cascade Books, 2019.

Smith, H. Augustine, ed. *Praise and Service*. New York: Century, 1932.

Springer, Carl P. E. "Reflections on Lutheran Worship, Classics, and the *Te Deum*." *Logia* 5.4 (1996): 31–43.

Stackhouse, Rochelle A. "Isaac Watts, Composer of Psalms and Hymns." In *From Catholic Europe to Protestant Europe*, edited by Mark A. Lamport, Benjamin K. Forrest, and Vernon M. Whaley, 197–209. Vol. 2 of *Hymns and Hymnody*. Eugene, OR: Cascade Books, 2019.

Sterk, Andrea. See Coakley, John W.

Tel, Martin. "Calvinist and Reformed Practices of Worship." In *Historical Foundations of Worship*, edited by Melanie C. Ross and Mark A. Lamport, 178–191. Grand Rapids, MI: Baker Academic, 2022.

Thurman, Kira. *Singing Like Germans: Black Musicians in the Land of Bach, Beethoven, and Brahms*. Ithaca, NY: Cornell University Press, 2021.

Tyson, John R. *Assist Me to Proclaim: The Life and Hymns of Charles Wesley*. Grand Rapids, MI: Eerdmans, 2007.

Vlhormá-Wörner. See Holeton, David.

Walsh, Peter G. with Christopher Husch, ed. and trans. *One Hundred Latin Hymns: Ambrose to Aquinas*. Cambridge, MA: Harvard University Press, 2012.

Watson, J. R. *An Annotated Anthology of Hymns*. Oxford: Oxford University Press, 2002.

Wellesz, Egon. *A History of Byzantine Music and Hymnography*, 2nd ed. Oxford: Clarendon, 1998.

Wesley, John and Charles Wesley, editors. *Hymns and Sacred Poems*. London: Wm. Strahan, 1739; facsimile edition, Madison, NJ: The Charles Wesley Society, 2007.

Westermeyer, Paul. *Hymnal Companion to Evangelical Lutheran Worship*. Minneapolis: Augsburg Fortress, 2010.
———. *Te Deum. The Church and Music*. Minneapolis: Fortress Press, 1998.

Hymnals

African American Heritage Hymnal. Chicago, IL: GIA Publications, 2001.
All Creation Sings: Evangelical Lutheran Worship Supplement. Minneapolis: Augsburg Fortress, 2020.
Books of American Negro Spirituals, The. James Weldon Johnson and J. Rosamund Johnson. New York: Viking Press, 1969; originally 1925 and 1926.
Evangelical Lutheran Worship. Minneapolis: Augsburg Fortress, 2006.
Glory to God. Presbyterian Church (U.S.A.). Louisville, KY: Westminster John Knox Press, 2013.
Hymns of the Breviary and Missal, The. Edited by Matthew Britt OSB. New York: Benziger Brothers, 1924.
Lutheran Book of Worship. Minneapolis: Augsburg Publishing House, 1978.
Lutheran Service Book. St. Louis: Concordia Publishing House, 2006.
Service Book and Hymnal. Minneapolis: Augsburg Publishing House, 1958.
Sound the Bamboo (The Christian Conference of Asia Hymnal). Manilla, Philippines: Asian Institute for Liturgy and Music, 1990.
This Far by Faith: An African American Resource for Worship. Minneapolis: Augsburg Fortress, 1999.
With One Voice: A Lutheran Resource for Worship. Minneapolis: Augsburg Fortress, 1995.

INDEX OF NAMES

INDEX OF HYMNS